The
BIG
BOOK
OF
MARTINIS

for
Moms

ROSE MAURA LORRE AND MAVIS LAMB
blogtender at FiveOClockCocktails.com

A adamsmedia
AVON, MASSACHUSETTS

Published by
Adams Media, a division of F+W Media, Inc.
57 Littlefield Street, Avon, MA 02322. U.S.A.
www.adamsmedia.com

Contains material abridged and adapted from: *The Everything® Bartender's Book,
3rd Edition*, by Cheryl Charming, copyright © 2010, 2007, 1995 by F+W Media,
Inc., ISBN 10: 1-4405-0383-4, ISBN 13: 978-1-4405-0383-2; *The Bartender's Guide*
by John K. Waters, copyright © 2006 by F+W Media, Inc., ISBN-10: 1-5986-9764-1,
ISBN-13: 978-1-5986-9764-3.

ISBN 10: 1-4405-5668-7
ISBN 13: 978-1-4405-5668-5
eISBN 10: 1-4405-5669-5
eISBN 13: 978-1-4405-5669-2

Printed in the United States of America.

10   9   8   7   6   5   4   3   2   1

Photography by Kelly Jaggers.

*This book is available at quantity discounts for bulk purchases.
For information, please call 1-800-289-0963.*

Contents

Chapter 4: Bathroom-Related Feats 71

Chapter 5: Transitions/First Feats 95

Chapter 6: School Feats 115

Chapter 9: Out-and-About Feats 173

Chapter 10: Festive Feats 191

Chapter 11: Kids Will Be Kids Feats 211

The Feat	The Reward	Page
Finally Broke Down and Got a Puppy	The Greyhound Martini	212
Hosted a Playdate	Key Lime Pie	214
Taught Your Kid to Play "Chopsticks"	Maestro	216
Let Your Kids Destroy the Living Room to Make a Blanket Fort	Beach Blanket Bingo	217
Changed Batteries in a Toy	The Fizzzbite	218
Helped Your Daughter Furnish Her Dollhouse	Bourbon Satin	219
Made Macaroni Art	American Sweetheart	220
Answered the Question "Why?" Umpteen Times in a Row	Jamaican Me Crazy	221
Named Girl Scout Troop Leader	The Thin Mintini	222
Attended Your Daughter's Tea Party	Electric Iced Teani	223
Let Your Daughter Do Your Hair and Makeup	Crown Jewel	225
Played House with Your Daughter and Let Her Be the Mom	Oatmeal Cookie	227
Watched Your Kids' Favorite Movie with Them	The Hollywood	228
Went on a Mother-Daughter Shopping Spree and Stayed on Budget	Park Avenue	230
Made It Out of the Store with the Year's Hot Brand-Name Toy	Dream Martini	231
Indulged Your Child's Wish for Their Bedroom Décor	Asylum	232

Chapter 12: In the Great Outdoors Feats 233

The Feat	The Reward	Page
Served as CEO of the Lemonade Stand	Lemon Drop	234
Got the Kids to Play Outside	Mudslide Martini	236
Survived a Jam-Packed Day of Soccer, Swimming, Etc.	Bloody Mary Martini	238

Introduction

Have you ever:

- Survived being up all night with a sick kid?
- Handled a diaper blowout without calling in the Hazmat team?
- Won the battle of the messy bedroom?

Of course you have! You're a mom and, while you love your role—and your kids!—you know for sure that parenting isn't the easiest job in the world. After all, a lot of what hard-working moms have to do isn't very glamorous and doesn't come with a paycheck, let alone much of a thank-you. Every day, you deal with temper tantrums, moments of panic, and the messiest messes imaginable, but despite the daily crises that occur around you, you also realize how lucky you really are to be surrounded by little ones who love you unconditionally. But that doesn't mean that, after a hard day, you don't sometimes want to mix up a nice strong martini, sit on the couch, and just take a deep breath and relax.

This is where *The Big Book of Martinis for Moms* comes into play! Here, you'll find more than 150 martini recipes, each tied to a specific feat commonly experienced in the life of a mom. So whether you've just given your newborn his first bath (the Bathtub Gin Martini), managed a mega carpool schedule (the Tijuana Taxi martini), or renegotiated your kid's allowance (the Cookie Monster martini) you'll be set to relax once you've conquered that particular parenting feat! In addition, you'll find martinis specifically aimed at scenarios where you've managed to carve out some precious time for yourself. If you actually made it to a girls' night out, reward yourself with a Cosmopolitan. If you successfully went on an adults-only weekend getaway, you'll want to indulge in a Charming Proposal martini. Or if you finally managed to get the house all to yourself, feel free to celebrate with the Dreamsicle Martini.

Not sure how to make a martini? Don't worry. You're too busy to take a bartending class and you don't need to have earned your TIPS certification to mix up the martinis in this book. All you need is a shaker, a martini glass (or two), some ice, and the alcohols and garnishes used in the recipes throughout. For most recipes, all you need to do is pour, shake, and serve!

So what are you waiting for? Chances are, you've conquered at least one feat today and it's time to sit back, relax, and shake your way through *The Big Book of Martinis for Moms*. After all, you've earned it! Enjoy!

Chapter 1
Bedtime Feats

Adults tend to relish bedtime because we spend so much of the day exhausted and needing a good nap. Your kids don't always look at it that way, so it can often be a challenge to get your household settled down for the night. The nightly battles you go through may run the gamut of bedtime stalling tactics, but they're all a part of your routine. It might be getting that colicky, fussy baby fed and rocked into a state of calm. It might be picking the right bedtime story and reading it just so (or over and over) until those little eyelids get droopy. The struggle might even start before getting tucked in with that child who always fights putting on his pajamas.

Whatever kind of crazy goes on in your house before the lights go out, rest assured that you're not alone. Mothers around the world are rocking, reading, cooing, and tucking in right there with you. And you can look forward to a number of relaxing, calming cocktails to help you settle in when it's finally your turn to jump under the covers. So, grab your martini shaker and enjoy. Just be very, very quiet . . .

Warm Milk Is the Trick

The Feat: *Got Through the Night Without Waking Up*

Getting your child to sleep is one of the biggest hurdles a mom can face, and you have to do it every single night! Some nights, sleep comes like a welcome gift and your little one nods off in just moments. But then there are those other nights. You know, the ones where sleep is a foreign language that your kid doesn't seem to speak. You rock, and sing, and coo, and lull, and . . . nothing. Then you remember the trick about warm milk and you fix a little for your tyke. Slowly but surely that warm, white broth does the trick, and before you know it (okay it took a while), your child is asleep. Now, what about you? You deserve a little something to lull you into dreamland. After all, you've worked hard all day, stayed up later than planned, and you have to get up early and do it all over again. Here's a great idea . . . an adult version of the same magic. Mom's Milk with a kick!

The Reward: *Mom's Milk*

Makes 1 martini

½ ounce vodka
½ ounce hazelnut liqueur
½ ounce crème de cacao
4 ounces cappuccino
Garnish: whipped cream (optional)

Pour the ingredients into a shaker half filled with ice. Shake and strain into a martini glass. Top with whipped cream.

Drive You to Drink

The Feat: *Lulled Baby to Sleep with the Ol' Drive-Around-the-Block Trick*

Putting a baby down for the night often requires a routine. Or maybe it just requires a route. A little late-night tool around town could be just the thing to make a fussy baby pass out fast. Whether it's the hum of the engine, the sound of the tires, or just the gentle movement as the car cruises down the road . . . who cares. It works. Once you're back home, and the baby is tucked in safe, a glass of milk punch—a Deep South creation that can be made with either brandy or bourbon—is sure to knock you out for the night as well. Unlike most milk punch recipes, this one necessitates sticking the drink in the freezer for a few hours to lend it a slightly slushy texture, which gives you all the time you need to drive that baby off to dreamland. So make this cocktail a part of your bedtime routine and dream sweetly every night.

The Reward: *Milk Punch*
Makes 1 martini

> 2 ounces bourbon or brandy
> 1 ounce whole milk
> 1 ounce heavy cream or half-and-half
> ½ ounce simple syrup
> Splash vanilla extract
> Garnish: grated nutmeg

Whisk together all ingredients, except nutmeg, in a freezer-safe container. Place container in the freezer for up to 4 hours. When ready to serve, give mixture a stir before pouring it into a chilled martini glass. Sprinkle nutmeg on top.

Milk Punch

Shake It Up Baby, Now

The Feat: *Sang Entire Beatles Anthology to an Up-All-Night Baby*

Having a "Hard Day's Night"? Need some "Help" with a baby who wants to do nothing but "Twist and Shout"? That's just "A Day in the Life" of a harried parent, of course, but here's a little something to keep your spirits up: Every time your baby babbles, "Koo koo kachoo," what she's really saying is, "She loves you, yeah, yeah, yeah"! Okay, all song titles aside, sometimes you have to pull out all the stops to get your little one off to dreamland. And if that means you have to sing every Beatles song you know, you'll do it. That's one of the great things about you, because even if you would never step up to sing karaoke with your friends, you'll croon your little one to sleep every night. So, once your golden voice has done the trick and you're sure the baby is out for the count, administer a little something to your tired vocal chords. The Yellow Submarine martini is the perfect encore to your Beatles cover show, so mix it up and sip yourself to sleep.

 The Reward: *Yellow Submarine*

Makes 1 martini

1½ ounces vodka
½ ounce white rum
½ ounce banana liqueur
Garnish: banana slice

Pour your vodka, rum, and liqueur into an ice-filled mixing glass and stir briskly for about 1 minute. Strain into a chilled martini glass. To garnish, cut a slit in the banana slice and perch it atop the rim of your glass.

Witching Hour's Brew

The Feat: *Managed to Get Your Kid to Sleep Through The Night!*

The achievement may be your child's, but you should totally go ahead and take all the credit for this monumental accomplishment. After all, it was you who swaddled him nightly, established a calming bedtime routine, read *Goodnight, Moon* to him twenty times in a row, and rushed to his crib side during all those 3 A.M. bouts of baby anxiety. And, you've basically been working toward this night since the day you brought him home. So, now that he's sleeping through the night, take a bow. Yes, you can also take a peek at him, but no touching. You want to be careful not to wake him up since getting him to sleep was your goal in the first place. Now, what will you do with all this free time? How about making a Le Minuit, an intriguing, modern martini named after the French word for "midnight"—an hour you've got all to yourself again. All you need is a little apple juice and syrup blended with white wine and absinthe to create the perfect late-night martini that's just for you.

 The Reward: *Le Minuit*

Makes 1 martini

1 ounce Sauvignon Blanc wine
½ ounce absinthe
1½ ounces apple juice
1 dash orange bitters
Splash simple syrup
Garnish: orange twist

Pour your liquid ingredients into an ice-filled cocktail shaker and shake vigorously for about 20 seconds. Strain into a chilled martini glass and drop in your garnish.

Anxiety Antidote

The Feat: *Got Through the Night Without Waking Up in a Paranoid Panic*

Remember that night when you awoke in a half-dream state and started digging through your bed sheets, convinced that your baby—not yet old enough to crawl—had somehow crawled underneath the covers? Or how about that recurring nightmare you keep experiencing, the one about the elephant stampede in your neighborhood, that always compels you to get out of bed and go make sure your child hasn't been trampled by pachyderm feet? You know these crazy dreams are just a symptom of a lack of sleep, but that doesn't make them any less real. And, why is it that they seem to hit you just as soon as you manage to fade off to sleep? Well, those horrible hallucinations may finally be a thing of the past. You just enjoyed an entire eight hours of sleep! In a row! (Okay, it was six, but who's counting?) With no catastrophes imagined or deaths foretold, it's like a dream in and of itself. Toast your newfound well-restedness with a creamy, dreamy cocktail, laced with just a little jolt of caffeine, in case you still need a little pick-me-up.

 The Reward: *The Insomniac*

Makes 1 martini

¾ ounce vodka
¾ ounce hazelnut liqueur
¾ ounce coffee liqueur
Shot of espresso
2 ounces half-and-half
Garnish: espresso beans (or—even better!—chocolate-covered espresso beans)

Pour everything but the garnish into an ice-filled cocktail shaker. Shake vigorously for about 20 seconds. Strain into a chilled martini glass and drop in espresso beans.

A Nip after Your Nap

The Feat: *Found Time for a Nap—for Yourself!*

"You'll sleep when the baby sleeps," is what everybody and their mother (including yours) told you when you were pregnant and worried about how you'd ever make it through the next eighteen years on five hours of sleep (total). But that advice is easier said than done. "Sleep when the baby sleeps" might work if (a) you could also fold the laundry when the baby folds his laundry, (b) you found time to file your taxes when the baby was busy filing hers, or (c) you manage to wash your hair when the baby washes his. That's why moms become so adept at taking five-minute power naps or sleeping standing up. Just the idea of grabbing forty winks on the sofa makes you want to smile, doesn't it? So however you managed to find time for a nap, congratulations! There's nothing more rewarding than laying down just because you're tired and allowing your body to drift off to the land of Wynken, Blynken, and Nod. To celebrate, here's a martini pepped up with coffee and orange flavors to get you going post nap.

The Reward: *The Orange Restorative*

Makes 1 martini

> **2 ounces dark rum**
> **¾ ounce triple sec**
> **Splash coffee liqueur**
> **Garnish: orange slice**

Pour your rum, triple sec, and coffee liqueur into an ice-filled cocktail shaker. Shake vigorously for about 20 seconds and strain into a chilled martini glass. Cut a slit in the orange slice and perch atop the rim of your glass to garnish.

The Sleepytime Mar-Teani

The Feat: *Outlasted Your World-Class Bedtime Staller*

Your child is the best bedtime staller in the county and puts you through your paces (and patience) every night. But you worked through every delay and tactic thrown at you and the result is nothing less than astounding. Your little one is asleep and there's still a bit of time left in your evening. Now is the time for you to fix a martini for yourself and enjoy the quiet. And wow, is it quiet. In fact, were the Parenting Police to storm in tonight, they'd be so stunned by your abode's eerie stillness that they might actually accuse you of feeding this tea-tinged cocktail to your child in a misguided effort to get him the hell to sleep already. Of course, that would never happen, because that would mean one less martini for you. But with its calming combination of chamomile and just a nip of liquor, this drink should have you dozing off to dreamland soon after your little one is tucked in his bed—which means another rare first: Mom's first full night of sleep since goodness knows when.

The Reward: *Relaxing Teatini Martini*

Makes 1 martini

1½ ounces gin
1 ounce Sleepytime (or just plain chamomile) tea
¼ ounce lemon juice
Splash something fizzy (sparkling wine, Prosecco, club soda, Sprite . . .)
Garnish: lemon twist

Combine gin, tea, and lemon juice in an ice-filled shaker. Shake vigorously for about 20 seconds. Strain into a chilled martini glass. Top with your splash of something fizzy and add garnish.

The Quiet Grasshopper

The Feat: *Got the House So Quiet You Can Hear Crickets Chirp*

Listen. Do you hear that? It's called peace and quiet. Can it be true? Are your children really all tucked in bed and sleeping? No more squabbling with each other. No more struggles to finish homework, brush teeth, or put on pajamas. You did it! Chores are done, kids are in bed, and you finally have some time to yourself . . . quiet time. You're so giddy you have to suppress a giggle. But, suppress it you must for fear of waking someone and losing this magical moment. As you collapse on the sofa, try to remember how you accomplished this mission impossible so you can repeat it again tomorrow. Wait! Is it too quiet? Should you be worried someone is up to something they shouldn't be? Perhaps, but before you do a last-minute check, revel in a quiet so wonderful you can hear the crickets chirp. Okay, so maybe there are no crickets, but you can still celebrate the silence. And, in lieu of any crickets, why not celebrate with a Grasshopper? The liquid kind, that is—one that's all minty and cool, with just a touch of chocolate. No blender noise needed, just measure, shake, and pour into a chilled martini glass.

 The Reward: *Grasshopper*

Makes 1 martini

| 1 ounce green crème de menthe |
| 1 ounce white crème de cacao |
| 2 ounces cream |
| Garnish: chocolate shavings |

Pour the green crème de menthe, white crème de cacao, and cream into a martini shaker filled with ice. Shake and strain into a martini glass. Garnish with chocolate shavings.

Grasshopper

Slip Into Something More Comfortable-tini

The Feat: *Got the PJs on Without a Fight*

Tonight was a magical night, one that you hope happens again and again. Maybe it was a sign your child is growing up, or maybe it was a sign of everyone being very tired. Regardless, when it was time to get ready for bed, you calmly but firmly said it was time to put on pajamas, and left no room for discussion. What happened next was amazing. When you pulled out the PJs, your little tyke gave an expected sigh, but no more. No begging for more time, no stomping of feet, and no squirming. Instead, you were able to get your kid out of school clothes and into night clothes without a battle. Is this your child? Is this your house? Are you dreaming? Are you wondering why you're not in Kansas anymore? Who cares! Without all the expected hassle, you've actually got some extra time on your hands. Enjoy it. Put your pajamas on early, make a drink, and grab a good book. What's the perfect drink for this fantasy land evening? The Ruby Slipper Sipper martini fits the bill because there really is no place like home.

The Reward: *Ruby Slipper Sipper*
Makes 1 martini

| 1½ ounces DeKuyper Hot Damn! Cinnamon Schnapps |
| Chilled apple cider, to fill |

Pour the cinnamon schnapps into a shaker with ice. Shake and strain into a chilled martini glass, fill with apple cider.

The Read It and Don't Weep-tini

The Feat: *Read the Same Bedtime Book Twelve Times Without Trying to Skip Pages*

Again? Yes, again! Your child loves repetition and can't get enough of her favorite bedtime story. You know it so well that lines from the book keep popping into your head throughout the day. Still, you love that little kid more than she loves that story. So, while you really needed to tackle that pile of laundry or stack of dirty dishes, you instead tackled your boredom and put on your best story-telling voice. In fact, you put on a few voices—one for each character—and read like it was the first time you two had shared this bedtime book. The resulting giggles and smiles made it all worthwhile. As you set the book aside and gave your goodnight kiss, you knew you'd be back with the same book tomorrow night. But, that's a battle for another day. Now it's time to relish your scholarly feat and indulge in a literary libation. Who better to bond with than Papa Hemingway himself? This lightly sweet rum brew, with a touch of citrus tang, is definitely a taste worth repeating.

The Reward: *Hemingway Daiquir-tini*
Makes 1 martini

1 ounce light rum	¾ ounce fresh lime juice
¼ ounce maraschino liqueur	Garnish: lime wheel
½ ounce grapefruit juice	Garnish: 1 cherry
¾ ounce simple syrup	

Pour everything but the garnish into an ice-filled cocktail shaker. Shake vigorously for about 20 seconds. Pour into a martini glass. Garnish with a lime wheel and a cherry.

Hemingway Daiquir-tini

Baby Burrito Margarita-tini

The Feat: *Mastered the "Baby Burrito" Swaddle*

The way those expert moms swaddle up their kids so there are no floppy ends on the blankets is like blanket origami. Or, for those who envision everything as food, it's a Blanket Baby Burrito! You've wondered how those Supermoms do it and practiced over and over. More often than not you ended up with a blob of blanket. But, today was your day! You mastered the art of swaddling and proudly displayed your tightly wound bundle of joy. Any mom out there understands the importance of this achievement and the value of a snug-as-a-bug-in-a-rug baby. Now that your wee one is warm, safe, secure, and ready for transport, you deserve to commemorate the moment appropriately. Since you now have a baby burrito, it makes sense to go south of the border for a cocktail creation, and nothing says celebration like an ice-cold margarita! It's like a party in a glass with a salted rim of extra fun. Sure, you can throw it all in a blender, but this round, save some time and just shake and pour.

The Reward: *The Margarita-tini*

Makes 1 martini

1½ ounces tequila
½ ounce triple sec
1 ounce lime juice or the juice of ½ lime
Garnish: lime wedge

Pour ingredients into a shaker half filled with ice. Shake well and strain into a salt-rimmed martini glass. Garnish with a lime wedge.

The Margarita-tini

Order Now Temptation Martini

The Feat: *Learned to Love 3 A.M. TV Infomercials*

Late nights—or rather, early mornings—are truly a part of your schedule these days. Sometimes you're up late because your child can't sleep and needs some special attention. Other times you're up watching late-night television because that's the only time you can get chores done. The problem is that you've found yourself hooked on those 3 A.M. infomercials. You're amazed that, even though you know those things are all hype, you can believe a product might actually do all they say it can do. That gadget really *could* replace every appliance in your kitchen, help you shed pounds, and be successful in real estate investment, all for just three easy payments of $29.95! You're not sure if it's the script writing, the music, or the ongoing repetition, but more than once you've had to stop yourself from pulling out your credit card and picking up the phone. So far you've resisted, and that deserves some recognition! Instead of ordering something in the next ten minutes, make yourself a rewarding Temptation Martini. The Scotch, Dubonnet, and anise blend will lull you back to reality with each sip.

The Reward: *Temptation Martini*

Makes 1 martini

3 ounces Scotch whiskey	1 teaspoon anise liqueur
1 teaspoon Dubonnet	Garnish: orange twists
1 teaspoon triple sec	Garnish: lemon peels

Pour Scotch, Dubonnet, triple sec, and anise into a shaker with ice. Shake and strain into a martini glass. Garnish with twists of orange and lemon peels.

Smarty Pants Martini

The Feat: *Read an Entire Chapter of a Grown-Up Book Before Falling Asleep*

The amount of adult information that reaches your brain these days is very limited. It's not for want of intellectual pursuits, but more for lack of time and lack of energy. You still read every night, but most of your current library is made up of nursery rhymes and picture books. But, that hasn't kept you from trying, which is why you have a stack of "grown up" books beside your bed. And last night you did it! You read an entire chapter of one of your books before the sandman came calling. You immediately felt more informed, more educated, and ready to have a grown-up conversation . . . if only anyone was around to have one with. In deference to your sneaking in some time for yourself and continuing to expand your mind, an Ivy League cocktail seems in order. Smartly mix up gin, vermouth, and blue curaçao for the Yale Martini, and enjoy the cocktail hour. By the way, for a busy mom, the cocktail hour is anytime you're done driving for the night and the kids are squared away.

The Reward: *Yale Martini*
Makes 1 martini

1 ounce dry vermouth
3 ounces gin
2 teaspoons blue curaçao
Dash bitters

Pour all ingredients into a shaker with ice. Stir and strain into a martini glass.

Chapter 2
Food Feats

Food, glorious food! When it comes to kids, food is vital, and eaters are picky, very picky. But you are an amazing mom who never tires of trying new and creative ways to feed your kids. And yet there are challenges, like feeding your baby those first bites of solid food and the ongoing battle of getting your kids to eat more vegetables. Not to mention the ongoing, never-ending process of planning dinner (every night, for ever and ever). So please accept the universal apology for any complaints about what you set before your children. And, while we know it's not what you prefer, we get it when you throw in the towel and just order a pizza!

That's why we wanted to provide you with some rewarding martinis to tempt your palate. From sweet chocolate temptations to good-for-you vegetables to classic peanut butter and jelly, there's something for every mood you're in and every taste bud you have in your house. And, none of these recipes require baking, broiling, frying, or boiling . . . just shake, pour, and drink.

Martini Mash-Up

The Feat: *Fed Your Baby His First Solid Foods*

Are you ready to become your child's personal chef? While parenthood is full of pitfalls and mistake making, making homemade baby food is super easy, and a super-easy way to kid yourself into believing that you have a grown-up handle on things. Once your wee one is eating some solid foods, you can create tons of good-for-you-fare by mashing, mixing, and mangling a variety of big people food. We're not talking steak here, but that probably doesn't come as a surprise. The focus is on fruits and vegetables that you can purée into perfection. Now this can take some extra time, so to reward yourself, be sure to try some options that will pull double duty. Here's a great example. The next time you mash up some banana for baby's nutritious dinner, you can multitask by fixing yourself a frozen banana martini at the same time. Now you have supper for your little one, and it's easy to mix up a fruity, tangy sipper for you. Now this is living!

The Reward: *Frozen Banana Daiquir-tini*
Makes 3 martinis

¾ ounce dark rum	1 medium–large overripe banana
¾ ounce light rum	1 cup ice
½ ounce triple sec	Garnish: lime peel or maraschino
1½ ounces lime juice	cherry
⅓ ounce granulated sugar	

Combine all your ingredients, except the garnish, in a blender. Blend on a low speed for five seconds, then blend on a higher speed (like purée) until contents appear smooth. Pour into chilled martini glasses and add your garnish.

Pretty Is as Pretty Does-tini

The Feat: *Negotiated a Full Serving of Food Into a Petulant Kid's Mouth*

How can little kids be so fast and so strong? When it comes to feeding your child, your tiny tot can whip her head around so quickly that you miss her mouth every time. And, let's not even talk about the strength she has for pushing the spoon aside. On nights like that, you'd be happy to get just one full spoonful of food into her mouth. Then you remember the trick of holding a baby so one arm is behind you while you're holding the other one. Out of the high chair and into your lap, your sweet cherub doesn't know what happened. But you did, and before you knew it, you hit your goal . . . a full serving of food was inside her, instead of on her bib. And, with a smile on her little face, she looks so very pretty. And the same goes for you . . . very pretty, or in other words, *muy bonita*! Cheer your feeding success with a little cocktail that looks and tastes pretty, the Muy Bonita Rita. Start by crushing up your child's remaining graham crackers to rim a martini glass. That way you'll get some food with your cocktail, which is *muy bueno*.

 ## The Reward: *Muy Bonita Rita*

Makes 1 martini

Lime slice	1 ounce sweet-and-sour mix
Crushed graham cracker	1 ounce half-and-half
½ ounce tequila	Garnish: lime slice
1½ ounces Licor 43	

Rub the lime around the rim of a martini glass, then dip the rim into a pile of the crushed graham cracker. Pour the tequila, Licor 43, sweet-and-sour mix, and half-and-half into a shaker of ice. Shake and strain into the glass. Garnish with a lime slice.

Manna from Heaven Martini

The Feat: *Got Your Kid Hooked on Table Food*

Transitioning from baby food to table food can take some time. Your little one is used to food being soft, creamy, and smooth. Now you're throwing crunchy, crispy, and chewy into the mix. Plus, the flavors of table food are more intense to a child's palate. That can mean some serious negotiations before your tot is completely hooked. But, once again, Mom, you persevered and made it happen. Your kid now eats just what everyone else at the table does, within reason of course . . . it's still probably too soon to try spicy hot wings. But still, another milestone has been reached that should be commemorated and honored accordingly. Cheers to your child for eating "grown-up food" and cheers to you for all you did to make it happen. You know *everything* you serve won't be eaten and experienced as if it were ambrosia. But just the fact that your little one is trying new things and is done with baby food is a little slice of heaven. So, raise a glass of liquid ambrosia and revel in your accomplishment. The sweetness of the applejack and brandy blend perfectly with the champagne, creating a nectar-like martini that is pure bliss.

The Reward: *The Ambrosia*
Makes 1 martini

> 1 ounce applejack
> 1 ounce brandy
> Dash triple sec
> Juice of 1 lemon
> Champagne (chilled)

Pour first four ingredients into an ice-filled shaker. Shake well and strain into a martini glass. Fill with champagne and stir gently.

Lucky for You Libation

The Feat: *Taught Your Kid to Feed Herself*

One day it had to happen, but you were beginning to wonder when. Surely you wouldn't be banned to a lifetime of feeding your kid, would you? No, it just takes some time. Like so many moms in the past, you started with that oat cereal that's the perfect size for little hands and little mouths. Plus, it's just good for them. You showed her how you did it and she watched intently. Finally, she had that "aha" moment, reached out, picked up that bite, and just popped it into her mouth. *Victory!* Quite pleased with herself, she did it again and again. Your life was about to change for the better because when your child starts feeding herself, you get just a little more time to do other things. Lucky you! This brings to mind the Lucky Charm martini . . . a perfect balance of luck and cereal. What could be better than that? So get out the martini shaker and get your leprechaun on, because it's cocktail time.

 ## The Reward: *Lucky Charm*

Makes 1 martini

> 1 ounce Tequila Rose Strawberry Cream liqueur
> 1 ounce white crème de menthe
> 3 ounces milk
> Lucky Charms cereal marshmallows

Pour the liquid ingredients into a martini shaker of ice and shake. Strain into a martini glass and add the Lucky Charms marshmallows on top.

Pour Me a Martini

The Feat: *Taught the Art of Pouring a Beverage*

Being able to pour your own beverage goes a long way in making a child feel less like a "baby" and more like a "big kid." It takes practice and patience, and the true belief that there really is no use in crying over spilled milk. You had the right attitude and you stuck by your little one as he tried again and again to get it right. You never scolded when glasses tipped over. You never got upset when those same glasses were missed completely, and beverages were poured directly onto the floor. You helped your boy learn something new and conquer a skill, which is probably why you're in the running for Supermom. Now, although he's still supposed to ask permission first, he can get his own beverage when he's thirsty. Has all that pouring made you a little thirsty? How about you whip up a pitcher of vodka martinis and pour one for all the adults? Normally, it's all about the James Bond "shaken, not stirred" philosophy. But with a pitcher, it's best to stick with gentle stirring, so be sure your liquors are chilled.

The Reward: *Martini Pitcher*

Makes 4 martinis

> 10 ounces vodka
> 2 ounces dry vermouth
> Garnish: 1–2 olives or a twist of lemon

Pour chilled (freezer works great) liquors into a glass pitcher and gently stir until blended. Pour into four martini glasses. Garnish with one or two olives or a twist of lemon.

The Vege-tini

The Feat: *Negotiated a Full Serving of Veggies Into Your Child's Mouth*

For months, you've pleaded in your best sing-song voice for your kid to try *just one bite*. Instead, you've only succeeded in providing healthy nutrition to his bib, his tray table, his smeared cheeks and the floor below. And now—finally!—he's stuck that BPA-free spoon where the sun don't shine . . . nice and proper in his mouth, that is! You're thrilled that he ate some veggies and hope it's not just a fluke. But even if it is, it's still the perfect occasion to remind yourself how easy it can be to pack some extra vegetable goodness into your own daily diet. You're usually grabbing a bite on the go. But as soon as you have a moment to stand by a martini shaker, whip up the Cucumber Martini and celebrate vegetables. A shot of fresh cuke juice in this martini, for example, delivers vitamins A, C, and K, plus potassium and antioxidants.

The Reward: *Cucumber Martini*
Makes 2 martinis

2 ounces gin
½ ounce triple sec or Cointreau
½ ounce lime juice
½ ounce simple syrup
3 ounces cucumber juice (you'll need a fruit and veggie juicer, or go to your local juice joint)
Garnish: cucumber wheel

Combine all ingredients except garnish in an ice-filled shaker. Shake vigorously for about 20 seconds. Strain into chilled martini glass. Add garnish.

Cucumber Martini

Have a Nice Day Martini

The Feat: *Made Food in the Shape of a Smiley Face*

You'll try almost anything to get your child to eat a complete meal, and sometimes that takes a lot of creativity. Unfortunately, the same idea doesn't work every day. That's why today's brainstorm was to make the food look like a smiley face. Personally, you may not enjoy eating a meal that can look back up at you, but kids tend to see things a little differently. So with a bit of imagination and patience, you crafted a breakfast buddy for your tot. Pancake face, oatmeal hair, banana slice eyes, and a strawberry smile all came together on the plate. The food was met with giggles and smiles, but then it was eaten bite by bite. Amazing! When you look back on this moment and reflect on another small victory, enjoy a cocktail that shows even more creative thinking. Use up those banana slices by making a sweet little concoction called the Chiquita-tini. It'll give you your own little smile for the rest of the night.

The Reward: *Chiquita-tini*

Makes 1 martini

2 ounces vodka
1 ounce banana liqueur
½ ounce amaretto
1 ounce lime juice
Garnish: sliced bananas

Combine liquids into a shaker filled with ice. Shake and strain into a chilled martini glass. Garnish with sliced bananas.

The Dressed Up Drink

The Feat: *Actually Enjoyed Dinner Out—with the Kid—Without a Meltdown*

Take a victory lap around the restaurant, or at least once around the parking lot before you leave. You did it! You had a nice dinner in a nice restaurant with your child. Everyone was on their best behavior and used—for the most part—proper manners. There were no meltdowns or temper tantrums from your kid (or you). And perhaps best of all, your table did not become the center of attention because you had to escort junior outside for a reprimand and reminder of appropriate public behavior. That could actually mean he's listening to you! That is the sweet taste of success and, very likely, it is more satisfying than your favorite meal. Now you can dream of being all dressed up and actually having some place to go, even if you don't have a babysitter. So, once everyone is safely at home and before you change out of your good clothes, start planning for your next outing while you sip on this dressed-up cocktail. A classic martini with a bowtie is the perfect salute to your formal-manners-training triumph. Let's hear it for Mom and raise your glass high—all in good taste, of course.

The Reward: *Tuxedo Martini*

Makes 1 martini

> 2 ounces vodka
> 1½ ounces dry vermouth
> ½ teaspoon maraschino liqueur
> 4 dashes orange bitters
> Garnish: lemon twist

Pour all ingredients, except garnish, into a shaker with ice. Shake and strain into a chilled martini glass. Garnish with a lemon twist.

Better the Second Time Around-tini

The Feat: *Made Dinner for the Family Entirely from Leftovers*

Whether it's "Stew with Stuff I Have" or "This-and-That Casserole," anytime you can clean out the refrigerator while filling up the family is a good thing. Like most of us these days, you hate to waste perfectly good food, and you don't always have time to get to the grocery store. So today, with just what you had on hand, you became a homemaking hero! You defrosted, warmed up, mixed together, and baked to perfection—all to create a heartwarming dinner from freezer, fridge, and pantry. A dinner, mind you, that everyone ate up, and enjoyed! So, now that dinner is over and the table is cleared, it's time to applaud your culinary accomplishment. How about trying the same thing with the liquor cabinet? Grab all those miscellaneous bottles with a drop of this and a drab of that in order to create a leftover libation. The Long Island Iced Teani, famous for moderately mixing lots of liquors (say that three times fast), is a great way to cap off your leftover evening. And the taste is so good it may make you come back and ask for seconds.

The Reward: *The Long Island Iced Teani*
Makes 1 martini

½ ounce vodka	1 ounce lemon juice
½ ounce gin	Cola
½ ounce light rum	Garnish: lemon wedge
½ ounce triple sec	

Pour all ingredients, except the cola, into a shaker filled with ice. Shake vigorously, then strain into a martini glass. Add cola to fill. Garnish with a lemon wedge.

Chopstick-tini

The Feat: *Taught Your Child to Use Chopsticks*

Finally, your child is willing to try more than just the egg rolls and fried rice at your favorite Chinese restaurant. Together, you explore the unique tastes of Cashew Chicken, Sweet-and-Sour Pork, and Beef with Broccoli while sipping hot green tea. But today . . . today was a banner day because this was the day your child mastered chopsticks. You know it's not an easy feat; it took you some time to get proficient yourself. But kudos to you for having patience while rice and chicken ended up everywhere but in her mouth. Who cares if she's still happier with the trainer version of chopsticks? It's about trying new things and not giving up! And her positive attitude is all because of your example. It may be a while before she's ready for Kung Pao Chicken and even longer before a meal at the sushi bar. Still, when the time comes, she'll be armed with chopsticks and ready to roll. So for now, enjoy the time together, and relish your child's chopstick mastery. To celebrate, why not sip on an Asian-style cocktail? Both tasty and pretty, this sunrise martini takes sake to another level.

The Reward: *Rising Sun*
Makes 1 martini

2 ounces sake
½ ounce grenadine
Orange juice
Garnish: lemon slice
Garnish: 1 maraschino cherry

Pour sake and grenadine into a shaker with ice. Shake and strain into a martini glass. Fill with orange juice. Garnish with a lemon slice and a cherry.

The Liquid Lunch

The Feat: *Packed Up Your Kids' Lunches—the Night Before!*

Did the time-space continuum just fold in on itself? Did you unknowingly learn how to stop time? Did you accidentally pass through a wormhole that somehow allowed you to bag up tomorrow's sandwiches, yogurt packs, and juice boxes an impossible twelve hours ahead of schedule? Now, if you could just remember exactly what happened in what order, there's a chance you can repeat this phenomenon again tomorrow night. Even better, imagine your morning no longer running in hyper-speed. You could sit down to drink your coffee. You could actually brush your hair before leaving the house. Or, you could not question your good fortune too much and just enjoy those extra minutes now. So, step away from the cutting board and enjoy your much-deserved downtime with a martini. This cocktail will likewise screw with your sense of reality because it tastes just like a peanut butter and jelly sandwich—and who doesn't like a good PB & J? Plus, it won't stick to the roof of your mouth.

The Reward: *PB & J Martini*

Makes 1 martini

> 1 ounce vodka
> 1 ounce hazelnut liqueur
> 1 ounce raspberry liqueur
> 1 ounce amaretto
> 1 ounce cranberry juice cocktail
> Garnish: handful of raspberries

Combine everything, except garnish, an ice-filled shaker. Shake vigorously for about 20 seconds. Strain into a chilled martini glass. Add garnish of your choice, such as a few skewered raspberries.

PB & J Martini

Make It a Delivery Martini

The Feat: *Gave Up on Making Dinner, Ordered a Large Pepperoni*

You try to do it all and do it all perfectly, but reality keeps getting in the way. Every once in a while, everyone has one of those days—the ones where nothing goes right, and what almost does go right, seems to take twice as long to do. There you were at dinner time with too many chores left to do, not enough food in the refrigerator, and a hungry family to feed. What's a mom to do? Admit when enough is enough! That's just what you did when you remembered that one night without a home-cooked meal was not the worst thing that could happen. Besides, the occasional special treat called pizza night is always received with cheers! And right now, a little cheering would do you a world of good. So, a large pepperoni pie was on the way to save the day, and you had a few moments to enjoy your kids. After dinner, when you get a few extra moments, you should enjoy this as well . . . the Pizza–Bloody Mary Martini. It's a traditional Bloody Mary with pizza goodies as garnish and rim. Let's all cheer for that!

The Reward: *Pizza–Bloody Mary Martini*

Makes 2 martinis

> **Parmesan cheese and red pepper flakes for rimming**
> **2 ounces vodka**
> **5 ounces Bloody Mary mix**
> **Garnish: 2 pepperoni slices**
> **Garnish: 2 cubes of mozzarella cheese**
> **Garnish: 2 green olives**

Rim martini glasses with a mixture of Parmesan cheese and red pepper flakes. Add the liquid ingredients to a shaker filled with ice. Shake vigorously and strain into the glasses. Skewer the pepperoni slices, cubed cheese, and olives to garnish the drinks.

Better Than Cake-tini

The Feat: *Baked a Cake with Your Kid*

School bake sale, neighbor's birthday, or just for the love of chocolate . . . you did it! You baked a cake with your child and lived to tell the tale. Sure you went through twice the amount of eggs you needed, because your mini-baker dropped the first two on the floor. But you can clean that up later. Right now you can bask in the glory of quality time spent with your Cake-Boss-Wannabe of a child mixing, pouring, baking, and icing. And the masterpiece sitting humbly on your favorite cake plate is better than good, it's done. Okay, maybe there are some cake crumbs showing through and maybe the whole confection leans a bit to the left, but right now you're not sure which is sweeter—the chocolate icing or the image of your kid with frosting on her nose. Savor the moment as your satisfied child is in the other room watching TV. And before she comes in for a snack, savor those beaters covered in cake batter! Or better still, let her have them while you indulge in a little chocolate cake grown-up style. Liquid love in a martini glass . . . the Chocolate Coco Martini.

The Reward: *Chocolate Coco Martini*

Makes 1 martini

2 ounces Bacardi Coco
1 ounce white crème de cacao
1 ounce cream
Garnish: flaked coconut and dark chocolate
Garnish: whipped cream (optional)

Shake all ingredients with ice. Strain into a martini glass rimmed with flaked coconut and dark chocolate. And, if you're craving a little "icing on the cake," squirt on a little whipped cream, if desired.

Chocolate Coco Martini

Melts in Your Mouth, Not in Aisle Five

The Feat: *Survived Your Child's First Supermarket Meltdown*

There's something about the way a child's screams echo along the aisles of a grocery store that makes a meltdown in such a locale irresistibly tempting to a little one. Okay, maybe your kid doesn't do it on purpose, but sometimes it sure feels that way. When those supersized tantrums occur, it seems there is no way to bring it to an end—no matter what you try. What's a mother to do? Well, when faced with such an unbearably embarrassing situation, there's no shame in abandoning your cart full of food and hightailing it out of there. Often, the moment you walk out of the store, the meltdown starts to cool down. But don't risk walking back in; you don't need the stress. Just buckle everyone up and calmly cruise out of the parking lot. After dinner, your nerves may still be shot. You've definitely earned both dessert and an after-dinner drink. Combine the two with a Brandy Alexander, an ice cream martini that knows how to melt down with decorum.

The Reward: *Brandy Alexander*

Makes 1 martini

> 1¼ ounces brandy
> ¾ ounce white crème de cacao
> 1¼ ounces vanilla ice cream (or your flavor of choice), plus a small scoop more for the float
> Garnish: grated nutmeg

Pour brandy and crème de cacao into an ice-filled cocktail shaker. Add 1¼ ounces of ice cream. Shake vigorously for about 20 seconds. Strain into chilled martini glass. Float a rounded spoonful of ice cream in the middle of the glass. Grate fresh nutmeg on top.

Keep Your Hands Off My Martini

The Feat: *Did Not Eat Your Child's Forgotten Snack*

You skipped breakfast and then missed lunch, so by midafternoon, you were hungry and looking for something to eat. You spied your child's forgotten snack on the counter and almost dove in head first. But, you made that mistake one time before. The look on your kid's face when he came back to claim his treat was not that of a happy camper. And you felt like a heel for gobbling his goodies. So, you stopped and stepped back. Rather than have a repeat performance of that disaster, you set aside his snack—including that crisp dill pickle that he probably wouldn't even eat—and you then went about finding a snack made just for you. Kudos for the willpower and for remembering hard-learned lessons. To go with your snack, how about a funny little martini called the Fickle Pickle? It's not really that sour, it's just green from the melon liqueur. That way you can have a pickle at least in name and still avoid the snack wars.

 ## The Reward: *Fickle Pickle*

Makes 1 martini

> 1½ ounces vodka
> 1½ ounces melon liqueur
> ½ ounce Crown Royal
> 1 ounce triple sec
> Sweet-and-sour mix
> Garnish: 1 cherry

Pour all liquid ingredients into a shaker with ice. Shake and strain into a martini glass. Garnish with a cherry.

The Clean-Plate-Club Cocktail

The Feat: *Ate Every Bit of Your Kid's First Kitchen Creation*

Your child is interested in cooking and wants to experiment in the kitchen by creating dishes that you get to sample. Don't you feel lucky to be the one person trusted enough to try your kid's secret recipe for salad dressing? And what exactly is the black stuff floating in your drink glass? Hmmm. . . . Well, being the stellar mom that you are, you put on a brave face and made sure you had some antacids nearby. Then you sat down and began eating whatever it was that had been put in front of you. Not only did you eat every bite, but when asked what you thought about your meal, you replied, "It's just the way I like it." Awesome! You were polite and caring—way to demonstrate good manners. Now a performance like that deserves some sort of award. One liquid "trophy" that comes to mind is the Pimm's Cup Martini, mixed with soda that can help settle your stomach. *Bon appetit*!

The Reward: *Pimm's Cup Martini*
Makes 1 martini

1½ ounces Pimm's No. 1	
Club soda, to fill	
Garnish: 1 lemon wedge	
Garnish: 1 cucumber slice	

Shake Pimm's in a shaker of ice to chill. Strain into a martini glass. Fill with club soda. Garnish with a lemon wedge and cucumber slice.

Chapter 3
Medical Feats

Don't you think moms could teach doctors a thing or two about taking care of kids? You are the one on the front lines for every cold, flu, cut, and scrape your children get, and you play the role of Dr. Mom quite well. You know how to make boo-boos feel better and soothe upset tummies better than anyone. You are the one your children come running to when they don't feel good, and they have complete faith in you to make everything better. If that weren't the case, why would so many adults say, "I want my mommy," when they get sick—and mean it?

But, we know all those first-aid sessions, endless trips to the doctor, and all nighters staying up with sick kids can wear you down. Sometimes moms need a little "medicine" to feel better, too. So these pages are filled with fun and feel-good cocktails like the Pain Killer, the Witch Doctor, and even the Reviver. Enjoy them in good health, but if you ever feel under the weather, just take two martinis and call us in the morning.

The All Nighter Martini

The Feat: *Survived Being Up All Night with a Sick Kid*

An "all nighter" used to mean one of two things: (1) a dusk-till-dawn study session, or (2) a raging, all-night party. As a mom, your new kind of all nighter bears only a slight resemblance. You may find yourself up studying Google results for "how to break my kid's fever," or there may be blood-shot eyes come morning due to lack of sleep. But regardless of the reason, you were not going to bed until your child was through whatever this was. Even if you tried to lie down and close your eyes, you wouldn't have been able to sleep. As a worried mom, you went into a state of awareness and wakefulness until further notice. The problem, of course, is on the other side of the crisis when you're operating the next day on zero hours sleep. Fortunately, this classic martini may be just what you need. According to historical folklore, the Reviver martini was meant to be imbibed before noon on those days when a morning pick-me-up proves essential. So feel free to follow the "It's 5 o'clock some-where" rule as necessary.

The Reward: *Reviver*
Makes 1 martini

> 1½ ounces cognac
> ¾ ounce calvados (AKA, apple brandy)
> ¾ ounce sweet vermouth
> Garnish: orange peel

Pour your cognac, calvados, and vermouth into an ice-filled mixing glass. Stir briskly for about 1 minute. Strain into a chilled martini glass and add your garnish.

Reviver

Take One at Ten, Two, and Four, and Call Me in the Morning

The Feat: *Stayed Home with a Sick Kid*

Remember that saying "life is what happens while you're making other plans"? That's what it's like when you wake up with your day fully planned only to find that you have a sick kid that can't go to school. Everything changes when the body temperature rises and the cold or flu takes over your house. After some initial diagnosis and confirmation that, yes, you're both staying home, you were on the phone. Quickly you changed every meeting, appointment, and deadline to make room for your becoming Doctor Mom. In your new—and hopefully very temporary—job you spent the day at your kid's bedside giving comfort the way only a mom can. Soothing words, cool cloths, soup, juice, and medicine were all dispensed with lots of love. While your little one napped, you stayed quiet and hoped you didn't catch whatever it was. Perhaps you could use a little medicine of your own. Some will remember that advertising gimmick that Dr. Pepper should be enjoyed at ten, two, and four each day. That may be great for the real stuff, but this version probably should not be enjoyed quite so often . . . even though it'll make you feel a lot better.

The Reward: *Dr. Pepper*
Makes 1 martini

1 ounce amaretto 2 ounces Southern Comfort Cola	

Pour amaretto and Southern Comfort into an ice-filled martini shaker. Shake and strain into a martini glass. Add cola to fill.

Catch Me if You Can-tini

The Feat: *Didn't Get Mad When You Caught "the Bug" from Your Kid*

You always taught your tyke that sharing was a good thing. You just forgot to clarify that sharing should not include anything involving a cold, flu, or other bugs. Of course, anyone who has kids knows that once your child brings home a bug, everyone in the household is going to spend some time with it before it leaves. So there you were, having just nursed your child back to health, down-and-out with the same illness. But you were a trooper, and you tried not to whine (too much) because you knew your kid didn't make you sick on purpose. Now your challenge was just to see how quickly you could get over this malady and get back to work. Everyone knows you need to drink lots of fluids when you're under the weather. So while you're okay with downing some juice, you started to wonder why only kids medicine is grape flavored. Why do adults have to "take their medicine" as it were, when it tastes so bad? So here's an idea: Mix your fresh cranberry and grapefruit juice with a little grape-flavored vodka instead. Try the Grape Seabreeze martini and you'll be back to feeling like yourself in no time.

 ## The Reward: *Grape Seabreeze*
Makes 1 martini

1½ ounces grape vodka
Equal parts cranberry and grapefruit juice, to fill

Pour vodka into a shaker with ice. Shake and strain into a chilled martini glass. Fill with equal parts cranberry and grapefruit juice.

Move Over Martini

The Feat: *Bunked with a Frightened Child for the Night*

You had just drifted off to sleep after another long, exhausting day. That's when the blood-curdling scream from your child's room woke you in a panic. As you rushed to her bedside, you heard her frightened voice recount her dream of monsters and things that go bump in the night. Knowing she'd never go back to sleep by herself, you did what you knew you had to do if anyone was going to get some rest. You sprawled out beside her, promised to stay all night and curled up under a shared blanket (with your feet dangling off the edge). As kids will do, she drifted right off to sleep. You, on the other hand, found sleep a little too elusive. If it wasn't the eye-level glow of the night-light, it was the poke of a pointy elbow, or the scratch of a sharp toenail. Your first thought? Those nails are getting trimmed first thing in the morning. Your second thought was, I deserve a reward for this! And you're right. The perfect solution is a martini with Madeira wine, known for its long shelf life, kind of like the long-lived memory of a scary nightmare.

The Reward: *Bad Dreams Martini*
Makes 1 martini

2 ounces gin
1 ounce Madeira
½ ounce cherry brandy
½ ounce orange juice
Garnish: 1 maraschino cherry

Pour all ingredients into a shaker half filled with ice. Shake well. Strain into a martini glass and garnish with cherry.

Bad Dreams Martini

The Sting-tini

The Feat: *Administered Bee-Sting TLC*

It's one of the main duties of a mom: making boo-boos better. The bee sting is often one of the worst because it always seems so unfair. Your child is just minding his own business when—zap—he's jolted out of his playtime by the sharp sting of a nearby bee. Even if you don't have to worry about an allergic reaction, the pain and swelling are not to be taken lightly. And after you've done your best first aid, there are tears to be dried and hugs to be given. Then, you scout the yard for hidden hives and share a few words of caution to avoid future mishaps. All better? Yes. So now that your kid is off and playing again, what about you? You need a little something to calm yourself after all that excitement. Maybe a nice cocktail to soothe yourself? Something to sip on while you gratefully realize all is well again sounds good, right? With a bit of a sly smile, you picture the ideal concoction for this moment. It is, of course, The Stinger martini. A unique blend of brandy and crème de menthe is, in fact, just what the doctor ordered.

The Reward: *The Stinger*
Makes 1 martini

2 ounces B & B or five-star brandy	
2 ounces white crème de menthe	

Pour ingredients into a shaker with ice. Stir and strain into a martini glass.

Panic Free Zone-tini

The Feat: *Survived the First ER Trip*

The good news was everything was going to be okay, but that first trip to the emergency room is hard to get through. You tried to take comfort in the fact that other mothers had been through the same thing, but it did little to alleviate the worry you had for your own child. The feeling of helplessness overwhelmed you, as you were stuck in the waiting room anxiously wondering when someone would come out to help your son. You had to hide your own fears and worries because you didn't want your boy to be any more scared than he already was. Finally, it was his turn to be seen, and the doctor's calm demeanor started to put you at ease. When it was finally time to go home, you were armed with prescriptions, instructions, and some much-needed assurance. After a stop at a drugstore, you had your child safely tucked into bed and it was time to let it all out. You probably need a little TLC yourself and the best prescription is the Pain Killer martini. The combination of rum, piña colada, and orange juice will have you restored to your supermom self in no time.

The Reward: *Pain Killer*
Makes 1 martini

1 ounce Pusser's Rum
2 ounces piña colada mix
½ ounce fresh orange juice
Sprinkle of nutmeg

Pour all liquid ingredients into a shaker filled with ice. Shake and strain into a chilled martini glass. Sprinkle with nutmeg.

Dirty Job Martini

The Feat: *Took a Child's Temperature—Ahem, Rectally*

Sometimes being a mom is just a dirty job because you always get stuck doing the things no one else wants to do, like getting an accurate temperature from your little one . . . rectally. Kids are squirmy enough but you had to get yours to roll over and allow you to "get the job done." The great thing is you did it! You wisely acted like it was no big deal and moved as quickly as you possibly could. Then you recorded the number so there would be no unnecessary re-checks. Now, your kid has gone back to sleep, and you need some recognition for another dirty job done well. The ideal drink to toast your efforts is one you'll enjoy with your tongue firmly planted in your cheek. Yes, it's the Hot & Dirty martini to the rescue. Flavored vodkas make this drink so much easier. You just shake pepper vodka, vermouth, and a little olive juice to make it as dirty as you want it. Giggle and enjoy.

 ## The Reward: *Hot & Dirty*
Makes 1 martini

3 ounces pepper vodka
½ ounce dry vermouth
1 teaspoon olive brine
Garnish: olive stuffed with pickled jalapeño pepper

Pour all liquid ingredients into a shaker with ice. Shake and strain into a chilled martini glass. Garnish with an olive stuffed with pickled jalapeño pepper.

Patience Is a Virtue Martini

The Feat: *Endured the Endless Wait at the Pediatrician's Office*

Lesson of the day is to always make the visit to your child's pediatrician at the end of the day when you have nowhere else to be. There's nothing worse than sitting in that brightly lit room waiting . . . and waiting . . . and waiting with your sick child. But, you handled it like a pro and practiced Zen-like patience as you read a two-year-old magazine about fishing or something equally boring to you, all while keeping your child occupied, unfussy, and tear free. Finally, you get called back into the small exam room, only to wait some more. At least there were different old magazines in there, but not as much to entertain your kid. She was just about to lose it (okay, you were, too) when the doctor finally came in to see you. Whew! That was close, but you did it. You didn't yell, scream, complain, or even cry; both you and your child were champs! Now that you're back home, you need a different kind of doctor to put you in a good mood. Try the Good and Plenty prescription of licorice-flavored sambuca and Dr. Pepper.

The Reward: *Good and Plenty*
Makes 1 martini

½ **ounce Dr. Pepper**
3 ounces sambuca

Pour the Dr. Pepper down the side of a chilled martini glass and then pour the sambuca in over the back of a spoon.

The Kept-Your-Cool Hot Toddy

The Feat: *Nursed a Child Through a Bout of Poison Ivy*

Kids love to explore and get into things, and sometimes they bring home something no one wants to keep. Like in the case of your little one who came home after a day of playing in a nasty patch of poison ivy. Unfortunately, that noxious, sneaky plant seems to be almost invisible until you're standing in the middle of it. Then, well, then it's too late . . . which is why you had a dot-covered tot as it were. It was your job to nurse your child through the uncomfortable experience and, once again, you came through with flying colors. From soothing baths to anti-itch medicine to keeping little hands from scratching away, you were on duty and on task around the clock. You also ignored all that empathy itching, because it's not fair if you can scratch and your child can't. Now that the worst of it is over, you deserve a little reward for being such a good nurse. For keeping your cool so well, why not enjoy a tasty Hot Toddy Martini? This soothing cocktail will help you relax and forget about your worries, including that urge to scratch.

The Reward: *Hot Toddy Martini*
Makes 1 martini

½ tablespoon fine sugar	Splash lemon juice
Dash ground cloves	1 ounce bourbon
Dash cinnamon	Garnish: 1–2 lemon wheels
2 ounces warm water	

In a room temperature, or warmed, martini glass, dissolve the sugar and spices in 1 ounce of the warm water. Stir. Add the lemon juice, bourbon, and the rest of the water. Stir well and garnish with lemon wheels.

Hot Toddy Martini

The Digit-tini

The Feat: *Soothed a Child Whose Fingers Got Stuck in a Door*

Your child was playing quietly in his room while you worked on chores around the house. Then you heard it . . . that blood-curdling scream that can only mean great pain. You ran as fast as you could to take care of whatever it was. Flying into his room you were at first relieved to see no blood, no major injuries. Through his tears you figured out his fingers got stuck in the door, and while nothing was broken, the pain was excruciating. You rushed him into the kitchen and applied an ice pack—okay, maybe you didn't have an actual ice pack, but a bag of frozen peas works wonders for things like this. With peas soothing the pinkies, you soothed your boy with hugs and reassurance that everything was going to be okay. Eventually the icy vegetables did their thing and the tears dried. He was "all better" and ready to go play, but you needed another moment to collect yourself and be grateful it was nothing more serious. How about a nice cool cocktail to ease the way? The Pink Squirrel martini for those pink little fingers sounds perfect.

The Reward: *Pink Squirrel*

Makes 1 martini

1 ounce Crème de Noyaux
1 ounce white crème de cacao
2 ounces cream

Shake all ingredients in a martini shaker half filled with ice. Strain into a chilled martini glass.

That Voodoo You Do-tini

The Feat: *Came Up with a Homemade Remedy for Baby's Hiccups*

You tried every remedy and trick you've ever heard of and nothing seemed to work. Your baby still had the hiccups, and you were both about to lose your cool. But, being the amazing mom you are, you did it. You discovered your own secret remedy to cure those annoying things and now everyone in the house is quiet and peaceful. What's the trick? Well, you're not yet sure if you're ready to reveal your top-secret skill. You know it will be coveted, and while you figure you will eventually share it with others, for now, you're basking in the glory (and power) of what you've learned. You are master of all things baby related. Well, you've got this one thing figured out at least. You should stand tall and proud and, before your head gets too big, have a cocktail to toast your talents. With this heady feeling, what martini could be better than the tantalizing Witch Doctor? I mean, your hiccup cure does seem a little magical and you are, as far as you know, the only one who has figured it out. So, get out the shaker and pour yourself a creamy, sweet treat.

The Reward: *Witch Doctor*

Makes 1 martini

1½ ounces brandy
2 ounces cream
¼ ounce dark crème de cacao
¼ ounce simple syrup
¼ ounce vanilla extract

Shake all the ingredients in a martini shaker with ice, then strain into a chilled martini glass.

The Big Belcher Cocktail

The Feat: *Banged a Burp from Kid's Tummy*

Kids usually have cast-iron stomachs and can digest things that most adults wouldn't put near their mouths. Still, there are times when even little tummies can get upset and need a bit of help. Usually, just like when they were babies, a good burp makes a kid feel better. Heck, it even works for moms. So you pick up your toddler and hearken back to the days when he wasn't even walking. You gently start to tap on his back and you rock him back and forth. It takes a little time and a firmer tap than before, but eventually, you induced a burp so loud it startled you. The cool thing is it worked, and your boy is off playing again. All that belly work got you craving something good for your tummy, something of the martini variety. Why not reach back in time, way before your boy was born, to the late '40s, and have a classic sparkling wine cocktail. The Bellini-tini martini (kind of sounds like "belly," doesn't it?) is a tasty mix of peach and Prosecco. Make sure everything is nice and chilled and enjoy the bubbles. It's okay if you burp a little, too.

 ## The Reward: *The Bellini-tini*
Makes 1 martini

1 ounce chilled white peach purée
Prosecco sparkling wine, to fill

Pour the purée into a martini glass and fill with Prosecco. Note: You can buy the purée or simply make your own by throwing a few slices of peeled peaches into the blender and hitting the purée button (about 10 seconds should do it). A lot of people use champagne and a peach nectar or liqueur, but this recipe stays true to the original 1948 concoction.

Safety First Martini

The Feat: *OSHA-Approved the Whole House*

It's not just your kids, but the kids from the neighborhood, too. All day, every day, running around your house and having fun. You have no problem with them playing at your place. In fact you like being able to keep an eye on everyone, but you worry about any safety hazards that the kids could get into. There's nothing like an accident and a trip to the emergency room to ruin a good day. So you pulled out a clipboard and wandered from room to room looking for loose boards, ruffled carpet, and exposed sockets. You did the same thing outside the house and in the garage, because kids will go everywhere. Once your list is made, and you've taken a quick trip to the hardware store, you set to childproofing your entire house. OSHA would definitely approve of your handiwork, and you can now rest easier. In fact, now you deserve a cocktail. This one may not be OSHA approved, but in honor of your due diligence in home maintenance, a Rusty Nail-tini is the perfect drink. The simple flavors of Scotch and Drambuie make for a rich, sweet sipper that is pretty handy to have on hand.

The Reward: *The Rusty Nail-tini*
Makes 1 martini

> **2 ounces Scotch**
> **1 ounce Drambuie**

Pour Scotch and Drambuie into a shaker half filled with ice. Shake and strain into a chilled martini glass.

The I Call Bull Shot Martini

The Feat: *Resisted Caving In to the Newest Kids' Health Fad*

Every so often you read an article, get an e-mail, or see some report on television that shouts about the latest and greatest thing for your child's better health. Whether it's vitamins that look like gummy candy or special drink boxes to give him extra energy, there's always someone talking about something. But you know that the best nutrition is good wholesome food, and you don't need to worry too much about all those processed, packaged products that mostly just lighten your wallet. That's why you refused—yet again—to cave in to another pint-sized health food craze. Good for you, Mom, for changing the channel, deleting the e-mail, or throwing out the flyer. You stuck to your guns and to what you knew was right. Better yet, you weren't afraid to call something bull when you knew that's what it was. That's why now is the perfect time for you to try the Bull Shot martini. This drink uses vodka and beef bouillon to shore up your strength for the next round of health-related hype.

The Reward: *Bull Shot*
Makes 1 martini

1½ ounces vodka
4 ounces chilled beef bouillon
Dash Worcestershire sauce
Pinch salt
Pinch pepper

Combine ingredients in a shaker half filled with ice. Shake well. Strain into a martini glass.

Chapter 4
Bathroom-Related Feats

Moms, from first baths to first dental visits, you take on a lot. It starts out with the basics of diaper duty, but that's just the beginning. There's also potty training, proper cleanup, and everything else that goes on down there. You are the one who handles the worst of it and who teaches your children all the proper procedures. You're also the one who makes sure teeth are brushed and hair is combed. And we know you've struggled, more than once, to get gum out of your kid's hair. No, we're not sure how she got gum back there either.

So, with all those bathroom duties, you need to get proper recognition, and this chapter gives you plenty of martinis to keep you calm and carrying on. From Bathtub Gin to the Pink Lady and the Gibson to the White Russian, you can shake and pour your way through whatever bathroom experience fills your day. Oh and we highly recommend, whenever possible, that you take one of these martinis, lock yourself in the bathroom, and enjoy a hot bubble bath.

The Number Two-tini

The Feat: *Handled a Diaper Blowout Without Calling in Hazmat Team*

What passes for proper cocktail conversation changes once you have a child, so let's cut the polite chitchat and discuss what's really on your mind these days—namely, those nasty nappies. Baby poop is, quite frankly, a surprise every time you encounter it, and not in a good way. While most diaper changes can be done quickly and cleanly, you just dealt with a doozy. A complete "odorific" blowout that tested your mettle, and you conquered it like a warrior. Now you know your gag reflex is in good working order and why you *always* carry a change of clothes for your baby. At least you'll have a few embarrassing stories you can share when your child is old enough to turn red around his friends. Since there's no getting around the fact of nature that is diaper changing, all you can do is cope. And coping is where your next martini comes into play. The Gibson, a classic dating back to the turn of the twentieth century, is simply a martini garnished with some stinky pearl onions because any good parental coping mechanism ought to contain a joke made about your baby's bodily functions, right?

The Reward: *The Gibson*

Makes 1 martini

> **4 ounces dry gin**
> **½ ounce dry vermouth**
> **Garnish: two or three pearl onions (also known as cocktail onions)**

Pour gin and vermouth into an ice-filled mixing glass. Stir briskly for about a minute. Strain into a chilled martini glass and add pearl onions, skewered or not skewered.

The Gibson

A Quick-Change Cocktail

The Feat: *Changed Your Baby's Diaper in a Parking Lot/National Landmark/Wind Tunnel/War Zone/Anti-gravity Chamber*

There's everyday diapering, which you can do (and have done, countless times) in your sleep—and then there's professional-level, extreme sports–style diapering, when you're suddenly forced to change your baby on the fly, in public, without such at-home creature comforts as a baby-wipe warmer, a distracting mobile, or an extra set of parental hands. So you put your MacGyver survival skills to the test and—presto change-o!—a magazine morphs into a changing pad, bobby pins stand in for your trusted Snappi, and those fast-food napkins in the glove compartment are pressed into service as not-so-hygienic-but-we-won't-tell-anyone wipes. Yes, Mom, you are that good, that quick witted, and that creative. Who knew the girl who used to be grossed out by a pimple could fly into action like that? You are awesome. Talk about daring; let's drink some absinthe! Seriously, absinthe is a liquor many avoid because of the rumors that you'll see little green fairies. Well, a mom who can change a diaper like that is not afraid of anything. So it's time to drink up!

 The Reward: *Absinthe Martini*

Makes 1 martini

---

2 ounces absinthe or pastis
2 ounces water
1 ounce simple syrup
Garnish: mint leaf (optional)

Pour absinthe, water, and syrup into an ice-filled cocktail shaker. Shake vigorously for about 20 seconds. Strain into a chilled martini glass. Add garnish, if desired.

Absinthe Martini

The Right Way to Wet Your Whistle

The Feat: *Managed to Not Get Soaked by Your Son's Mid-diaper-change Projectile Pee Pee*

Here's a tip that's got nothing to do with making cocktails, but does concern liquids that may wind up in your mouth. When changing your newborn son's diaper, try holding a second, clean diaper a few inches above his wee-wee during those moments when he's fully exposed. Little boys have been known to pee upwards while atop the changing table, and all babies have a knack for knowing the precise moment you need at least one hand free to brush the ick off your teeth. So, act like a Boy Scout (or Girl Scout) and always be prepared. If you realize too late that you forgot to put on that second diaper, be ready to bob and weave like Rocky in order to avoid the shower. And, when you're done, whether you managed to avoid the spray, or need some disinfectant, you deserve a good drink. So, why not try the Fog Cutter Martini. While you're not cutting through any actual fog, it's a stiff cocktail with enough alcohol to cut through whatever landed in your mouth and completely sterilize your contaminated kisser . . . plus it's pretty dang tasty.

 The Reward: *Fog Cutter Martini*

Makes 2 martinis

2 ounces white rum	½ ounce orgeat (almond-flavored
1 ounce cognac	syrup)
¾ ounce dry gin	½ ounce dry sherry
2 ounces orange juice	Garnish: 2 orange wheels
1 ounce lemon juice	

Pour all ingredients, except garnish, into an ice-filled cocktail shaker. Shake vigorously for about 20 seconds, then strain into chilled martini glasses. Cut a slit in the orange wheels and perch 1 on the rim of each glass to garnish.

A Tipple for a Tinkle

The Feat: *Endured the First Day of Potty Training*

Parenthood changes a person. One day you're a sane, rational grownup who interacts with others calmly and sensibly. The next, you embark on the arduous, thankless task of toilet training a toddler, and suddenly you're kneeling on the unforgiving tile of the bathroom floor, cutting deals with a stubborn three-year-old. You find yourself swearing you'll make ungodly amounts of candy magically appear in exchange for just one itty-bitty poopsie or little peepsie in the potty. Don't worry, years later you'll be able to look back and laugh. It may be quite a few years, but it will happen. After your potty talks, you may feel the urge to stare into the bathroom mirror, searching for the person you once were—the one who used to have intellectual conversations with real grownups. The one who—you're pretty sure—never talked about going to the bathroom, at least in any detail. Instead of soul searching, just head straight to the liquor cabinet, and mix the new you a martini that speaks to the hit-or-miss-ness of toilet training, not to mention your newfound personality.

 ## The Reward: *Dirty-Dry-Dirty Martini*
Makes 1 martini

2 ounces dry gin
¼ ounce dry vermouth
Splash lime juice
Splash olive brine
Garnish: skewered green olives
Garnish: lemon twist

Pour your gin, vermouth, lime juice, and brine into an ice-filled cocktail shaker. Shake vigorously for about 20 seconds. Strain into a chilled martini glass and add garnish.

A Drink for Poo— Who Knew?

The Feat: *Taught Your Child How to Wipe*

To make waste is human; to wipe, divine. At least, that's how it feels to a potty-training parent. Oftentimes, teaching your tot to clean his bottom after a bathroom visit proves to be a completely separate—and damn trickier—endeavor than just getting him to sit on a toilet seat and do his business in the first place. In fact, did you know that sometimes a child's arms aren't yet long enough to reach down there? Your kid may tell you this, and you may think it's just a ploy, but it's really true. So, practice your patience and keep on wiping. Remember, you figured it out at some point and your child will too. At times it may seem unbelievable—but almost as unbelievable is the fact that the Pooh'tini is an actual cocktail, invented at a popular New York City club in the late '90s. Don't worry; it gets its name from the honey liqueur that's used and nothing else. So when you get out of the bathroom, remember to wash your hands. Then head to the liquor cabinet to mix up this sweet treat.

 ## The Reward: *Pooh'tini*
Makes 1 martini

> 2 teaspoons honey
> 2 ounces vodka
> ½ ounce honey liqueur
> 1½ ounces cold chamomile tea
> Garnish: lemon twist

First, dissolve the honey a bit by stirring it with the vodka in the bottom of a cocktail shaker. Then add your liqueur, tea, and plenty of ice and shake vigorously for about 20 seconds. Strain into a chilled martini glass and drop in your garnish.

Pooh'tini

Close-the-Commode Cocktail

The Feat: *Taught Your Son Not to Leave the Seat Up*

The rule says that when a boy is finished in the bathroom, he must return the toilet seat to its rightful, lowered position. After all, you don't want to suffer the eau de toilette–wetted butt cheeks that come when the seat is left up. Unfortunately, this is a thing that most guys just don't understand, and so this bit of etiquette often falls to Mommy to instill. Of course, your boy may offer the same response adult males do, "Why don't you just look before you sit down?" But, breathe through your initial reaction and put on your Ms. Manners hat to explain, yet again, why this is just how it's done. Eventually, he'll get the message—even if he doesn't practice it every time. When you finally get the nod of understanding, it's time for a reward—for you that is. The ideal martini for the moment has got to be the Cheeky Monkey, as a toast to having dry cheeks forever more, you hope. This citrusy vodka martini will put a smile on your face every time.

The Reward: *Cheeky Monkey*
Makes 1 martini

1 ounce citrus-flavored vodka (like Absolut Citron or Ketel One Citroen)

1 ounce yellow Chartreuse

2 ounces orange juice

1 dash orange bitters

Garnish: orange twist

Pour your liquid ingredients in an ice-filled cocktail shaker. Shake vigorously for about 20 seconds. Strain into a chilled martini glass. Drop in your garnish.

Sip 'n Sin

The Feat: *Caught Your Kid Touching "Down There," Didn't Freak Out*

Ah, hormones. They may rear their ugly little heads as early as infancy (when babies still have a lot of Mom's reproductive juices left in their systems), or they may lay dormant awhile before making a big splash during preadolescence (a phase that, science shows, is starting to kick in at a younger and younger age). During either stage of life, the unfortunate day may come when you inadvertently witness your offspring treating his or her nether region like a Tickle Me Elmo doll. Wig out a little bit, by all means, but there's no need to totally come unglued. Just try not to have your freak out in front of your kid. Remember, it's all perfectly normal and natural, and it's not like your kid even realizes he or she is doing it. So use the time to have an age-appropriate conversation about what we do in public and what we do during private time. And, for this conversation, less is always more. You know that "touching down there" isn't a sin, but you know what is really sinful? The Gin and Sin, a delicious, syrupy, citrusy, sweet martini that'll help calm you down.

The Reward: *Gin and Sin*

Makes 1 martini

> 2 ounces dry gin
> 1 ounce orange juice
> ½ ounce lemon juice
> Splash grenadine syrup (or, as a sub, maraschino cherry juice)
> Garnish: orange twist

Pour your gin, juices, and grenadine in an ice-filled cocktail shaker. Shake vigorously for about 20 seconds. Strain into a chilled martini glass and drop in your garnish.

The Squeaky Clean Martini

The Feat: *Gave the Baby a Bath*

Preparenthood, certain activities were undertaken for the life-and-death thrills they provided: skydiving, running with bulls, eating a hot dog from a gas station. Now, when jonesing for a euphoric high coupled with the terror of the unknown, simply give your newborn a bath. Babies are usually as happy and content (and adorable!) in the tub as you are petrified of them being there. Remember, before birth, babies were basically aquatic for nine months. So breathe deep and work quickly from the head down, using a baby-soft washcloth and lukewarm water. If you're really nervous, skip the tub altogether and go for a little rubber tub that can fit into the kitchen sink. It works wonders to keep you in control. Oh, and until the baby's old enough to ask for one, a bubble bath's not necessary, so save the fragrances, florals, and whatnot for later. For now, it's time for a postbath martini that's good and clean. Don't worry about using actual bathtub gin, just shake, pour, and enjoy.

The Reward: *Bathtub Gin Martini*

Makes 1 martini

4 ounces gin
1 ounce dry vermouth
2 dashes orange bitters
Garnish: lemon twist

Pour gin, vermouth, and bitters into an ice-filled mixing glass. Stir briskly for 1 minute and strain into a chilled martini glass. Add your garnish.

The Cocktail Files

The Feat: *Gave Baby's First Manicure Without Getting Scratched in the Face*

Hopefully someone warned you that a baby's fingernails are like insane little flesh-cleavers before a part of your face found out the excruciatingly painful way. Perhaps it's because they're so tiny and thin, but those razor-sharp fingernails can do some real damage. In fact, infants have been known to scratch their own corneas, so giving your little one a manicure is a must-do from very early on. Do it while the baby is sleeping to avoid any unnecessary trauma, for either of you. If using a pair of specially-sized nail clippers is more than you can handle, you can just file those claws down using the soft side of an emery board. It won't take long, but you'll be glad you did it. When your time as a manicurist is over, reward yourself for pulling off such a fearsome feat with a Pink Lady, a classic, pre-Prohibition martini that, like your little Wolverine, hides a sharp taste behind a pinkish hue of cuteness. The egg white brings a softness to the gin, juice, and grenadine blend.

The Reward: *Pink Lady*
Makes 1 martini

2 ounces dry gin
½ ounce lemon juice
¼ ounce grenadine
Egg white from a medium-sized egg
Garnish: 1 lime wedge
Garnish: 1 maraschino cherry

Combine all ingredients in a cocktail shaker that doesn't have any ice in it. Shake vigorously for about 20 seconds, then fill shaker with ice and shake for another 20 seconds. Strain into a chilled martini glass and garnish with lime wedge and maraschino cherry.

Pink Lady

The Walking Wounded Cocktail

The Feat: *Didn't Freak Out When You Saw Your Child's Bloody Wound*

Kids get hurt a lot, but they bounce back pretty quickly. However, it's a lot harder for moms to bounce back when they first see a bloody wound on their child. When your child came home needing some immediate first aid, you remembered that if he saw you freaking out, he might freak out too. So you swallowed hard and focused on the task at hand. After a good cleaning, it was clear that the cut wasn't as bad as it first appeared. So you patched him up with ointment and bandages, and he felt good enough to go back outside to play. You still felt a little queasy and knew that image of his banged-up leg would stick in your mind for quite some time, but you were proud of yourself for keeping cool and playing the role of nurse to a T. With your boy on the mend, you now need a little medicinal support to soothe yourself. What better cocktail than the classic Blood and Sand martini to help you remember and forget at the same time?

The Reward: *Blood and Sand*
Makes 1 martini

1 ounce Scotch whiskey
1 ounce Cherry Heering
1 ounce sweet vermouth
1 ounce orange juice

Pour ingredients into a shaker with ice. Shake and strain into a martini glass.

Sticky Business Martini

The Feat: *Got Gum Out of Your Kid's Hair*

No one's ever quite sure how it gets there, but once it's there, it doesn't want to leave. We're talking, of course, about gum in the hair. Typically there's some sort of a bubble gum blowing mishap involved, but who knows. The real issue of course, is the herculean effort needed to remove it. That's followed closely by the question of why does it always seem to happen late at night before picture day? Still, no matter when or how it happened, you managed to get that gum out without losing too much hair in the process! Through all the tears and screams that you were torturing her, you carefully oiled and peanut buttered your kid's hair to freedom. Maybe you had to snip a bit here or there, but for the most part all the tresses are still intact and a good shampoo will get her hair back to normal. While she's finishing her homework or otherwise occupied, now it's time for your reward. And, what a sweet reward it is . . . a yummy bubblegum-flavored cocktail. And, it tastes so good you won't risk spilling a single drop in your hair or anywhere.

The Reward: *Bazooka Joe Martini*

Makes 1 martini

1½ ounces Irish cream
1½ ounces blue curaçao
1½ ounces banana liqueur

Pour all ingredients into a shaker with ice. Shake and strain into a martini glass.

Bazooka Joe Martini

The Edward Scissorhands Cocktail

The Feat: *Combed Your Child's Hair Into Something Resembling a Hairstyle*

Why is it always right before school that your child's hair decides not to cooperate with you? With just five minutes to comb that cowlicked mess into something that looked like a hairstyle, you channeled your inner Vidal Sassoon and hoped for the best. Of course, it didn't help that your client would not sit still and kept wiggling out of your reach. Hold tight, Mom, and hang tough. Just when you're about to get out the clippers and take care of the problem for good, all those spikey hairs settled down. It was almost as if the hair knew its days were numbered and started to behave. At least you could send your child off to school without a shaved-down dome. Now you deserve a little something to reward your restraint in clipper use on a minor. How about a twist on the Fuzzy Navel . . . the Hairy Navel martini? Oh, and before you do that, you might want to make an appointment with your own hairdresser.

The Reward: *Hairy Navel*
Makes 1 martini

1 ounce vodka
1½ ounces peach schnapps
Orange juice

Pour the vodka and schnapps into a martini shaker half filled with ice. Shake vigorously and strain into a martini glass. Add orange juice to fill.

Ooh La La Hairdo-tini

The Feat: *Figured Out French Braids for Your "Do-Obsessed" Daughter*

Maybe you've never been one for fancy hairdos. Or if you are, maybe you've always had someone else create your styles. But when you had a daughter, you became a hairstylist whether you wanted to or not. From baby bows to pigtails, you've learned how to create looks pulled right from the magazines . . . or at least you've tried to. You just conquered one of the more elusive looks, the French braid . . . Mom of the Hour! For years, a regular braid would satisfy her just fine, but no more. Your sweet girl has become hairdo obsessed and wanted a more grown-up look. You were willing to oblige and learn some new tricks, but while it's not as easy as it looks, after a trial period wrought with frustration, retries, and sore arms, you finally figured it out. And while your daughter is showing off her new look to her friends, you need to celebrate. So break out the bubbly and enjoy . . . as soon as your arms have rested enough to pick up the martini shaker.

The Reward: *French 75*

Makes 1 martini

> 1 ounce gin
> 1 ounce lemon juice
> ½ ounce simple syrup
> Champagne
> Garnish: 1 lemon twist

Pour the gin, lemon juice, and simple syrup into a martini shaker half filled with ice. Shake vigorously and strain into a martini glass. Add champagne to fill and garnish.

French 75

The Breath Freshener

The Feat: *Survived the First Trip to Dentist*

It's only a checkup, but it's a first checkup . . . and it's at the dentist's office? Even you don't like to go to the dentist—who does? Still, you're the mom and you want to make sure your kid has good, healthy teeth. So making light of your own issues with the tooth tormentor, you assure your child there's nothing to be afraid of and head out the door. Everything was great until you were in the waiting room and heard that eerie sound of a drill. Your kid's eyes widened into saucers and filled with fear and, well, horror. It's make or break time here, Mom. With a reassuring arm around your child, you soothingly say there's nothing to worry about. You're just here to let the dentist have a look at your choppers and to get some tips on proper brushing. Brilliant thinking! Fears subside, the checkup goes just fine, and your child actually likes that postcleaning minty fresh flavor. Minty fresh? That's a great idea for a rewarding cocktail. Blend a little chocolate liqueur with peppermint schnapps and enjoy!

The Reward: *Adirondack Mint*
Makes 2 martinis

> 1 ounce Godiva Chocolate Liqueur
> 1 ounce peppermint schnapps
> 2½ ounces hot chocolate, cooled to room temperature
> Garnish: whipped cream

Pour all ingredients into a pitcher and gently stir. Pour into martini glasses. Top with whipped cream.

The Tell the Tooth-tini

The Feat: *Played Tooth Fairy*

Your baby is growing up, whether you're ready for it or not. One of the telltale signs is losing baby teeth, and your little one had just lost her first one. There you were faced with the reality of aging *and* with the knowledge you had to play tooth fairy! Maybe you're not very good at keeping secrets and stealthy activities were never your cup of tea, but no matter what, you're going to create a visit from the winged fairy of all things dental. Forget an IOU written on a sticky note; you, oh fabulous Mom, are prepared. You had the perfect amount of money, maybe a cute little money bag, and patience. You waited up until your child was sound asleep, despite being oh-so-sleepy yourself. Then, with ninja-like moves, you silently and quickly made the magic exchange. And with the tooth safely tucked away, you realize you need to celebrate. Before you tuck yourself into bed, what about a little something to honor your kid's incoming pearly whites? What better to imbibe than a creamy, sweet White Russian Martini? A perfect blend of vodka, coffee liqueur, and cream—and then off to bed. Just don't forget to brush your teeth!

 The Reward: *White Russian Martini*

Makes 1 martini

1 ounce vodka
1 ounce coffee liqueur
2 ounces cream
Garnish: espresso beans (optional)

Pour all ingredients into a shaker of ice and shake. Strain into a chilled martini glass. Top with espresso beans.

White Russian Martini

The Million Dollar Smile

The Feat: *Ponied Up for Braces*

Beauty isn't everything, but you still wanted your kid to have nice, straight teeth. But didn't it seem like every month, just when you thought you had your budget under control, something happened to change that? If it wasn't your car, it was a must-do house repair, or in this case, something your child really needed. You knew it wasn't just a cosmetic thing and, of course, you were *going* to get your kid the braces, but first you had to get over the sticker shock. How can such a little bit of metal cost so much? And then there were all the visits to the orthodontist that had to be calculated. At any rate, you figured it all out and scheduled that first appointment to get started. One step at a time is always the best way. Who knew, maybe you'd win the lottery soon and it wouldn't matter. Okay, maybe not, but you can at least live in that fantasy world a bit longer. Congratulate yourself on making it work out and helping your kid have a better future . . . and a better bite. Mix yourself the Million Dollar Martini, a cocktail worth its weight in gold, and keep on smiling.

The Reward: *Million Dollar Martini*

Makes 2 martinis

1½ ounces gin
1 ounce sweet vermouth
1½ ounces pineapple juice
½ ounce fresh lemon juice
1 ounce cream
¼ ounce simple syrup
¼ ounce grenadine

Shake all ingredients with ice and strain into martini glasses.

Chapter 5

Transitions/ First Feats

There's nothing like the first time something happens with your child. There are exciting firsts, like baby's first steps and first words, and there are awkward firsts, like when you have to sit down and talk to your child about the birds and the bees. There are rites of passage you'll go through, like when your son learns to ride his bike without training wheels or when you get your daughter her first cell phone. Regardless of the mood, these firsts and transitional experiences stay with you forever and are the memories that you will recall many years from now.

Each first deserves to be commemorated and honored in some way. This chapter gives you the martinis to help you do just that. You might find some recipes you'll be trying for the first time (the Peppertini or the Opera Martini), but you'll also find some classics you can enjoy in a new light (the Salty Dog and the Sidecar Martini). The important thing is to enjoy the firsts in your life and raise a glass high. Salud!

The Dirty Shirt Martini

The Feat: *Threw Away Your First of Many Perfectly Good Shirts*

News flash: Once you're burping a newborn after every feeding (that's eight to twelve times daily), you no longer own any "perfectly good shirts." Those things you wear to clothe your upper body are now merely spit-up rags waiting to be ruined. Yes, you could drape a proper spit-up rag (like a clean, prefolded diaper) across your shoulder to protect your garments, and those will catch the smaller messes. The thing is, babies don't always—in fact, they rarely—burp on demand. Also, a baby's burp often entails a stomach-vacating geyser, so voluminous, you may be tempted to have your baby checked for poltergeists. And, it will seem that you can never find one of those burp rags when the baby needs to be burped. So use 'em if you got 'em, but keep on burping! Nobody said this parenting business wasn't messy. That's why you deserve a reward and the cocktail most apropos has got to be the Dirty Martini. The level of "dirty" is up to you.

The Reward: *Dirty Martini*

Makes 1 martini

> 2 ounces gin
> ½ ounce dry vermouth
> ½ ounce olive brine
> Garnish: green olives, skewered on a swizzle stick, if you like

Pour your gin, vermouth, and brine into an ice-filled cocktail shaker. Cap shaker and shake vigorously for about 20 seconds. Strain into a chilled martini glass and garnish.

Say Cheese-tini

The Feat: *Discovered Your Baby's Inner Flirt*

So you've started to get the hang of this whole motherhood thing. The problem is that the routines you and your baby seem to be settling into still leave you confused, frustrated, and exhausted. A baby that falls asleep ten minutes after nursing, only to wake up and want to nurse again? A forty-five minute backrub to elicit just one burp? No parenting book prepared you for such craziness. Here's the freaky thing about kids. You can try to resent them from time to time, but they always know how to melt your heart at just the right moment. To wit: baby's first smile. It will arrive moments before you are ready to completely lose it, and suddenly you will realize, my baby just smiled at me. Smiled! At me! Not anyone else! She looked, she recognized, she smiled. And you are delighted. And, like any good first, it deserves to be celebrated and commemorated. So, belly up to your in-home bar and fix yourself your just desserts. This perfect moment calls for a martini that uses both dry and sweet vermouth . . . martini perfection.

The Reward: *Perfect Martini*
Makes 1 martini

1 ounce dry gin
1 ounce dry vermouth
1 ounce sweet vermouth
1 dash orange bitters
Garnish: orange peel

Combine your ingredients, except garnish, in an ice-filled mixing glass. Stir briskly for about 1 minute, strain into a chilled martini glass, and add your garnish.

Make Me Laugh More-tini

The Feat: *Discovered Your Baby's Inner Comedian*

Why does an infant's laughter feel even more precious than that first smile? While a smile can be chalked up to instinct (babies imitate the facial expressions they see you make, after all), a laugh is your first glimmer into the personality that's growing inside this tiny little person. "Anybody home in there?" is what you may have been tempted to ask in weeks past. Finally, a reply! You did something that made your baby laugh. A giggle from your child will turn you into a goofball as you try again and again to elicit the laughter. It's like nectar from the gods and you want more. This is indeed a perfect moment and deserves the ideal recognition. That's why it's time for the More Perfect Martini. So what makes the More Perfect Martini even more perfect than a Perfect Martini? Depending on individual tastes, you may find that the extra bitters in the More Perfect Martini make it taste a little more "fun." And fun is exactly what is needed to mark this milestone occasion of good humor.

The Reward: *More Perfect Martini*
Makes 1 martini

1 ounce dry gin
1 ounce sweet vermouth
1 ounce dry vermouth
3 dashes old-fashioned bitters
3 dashes orange bitters
Garnish: orange or lemon peel

Combine gin, vermouths, and bitters in an ice-filled mixing glass. Stir briskly for about a minute. Strain into a chilled martini glass, and add your garnish.

Sip Service or Let 'Er Sip

The Feat: *Got Your Kid to Drink Out of His First Sippy Cup*

A sippy cup is like a pair of training wheels for a glass. And getting a kid to get the hang of one can be harder than it looks. (Hint: Some moms admit to resorting to chocolate milk—gasp!—to make sippy cups more attractive.) Still, it is one of those things that you know your kid will (has to) get the hang of sooner or later. So, you just keep working and practicing with your wee one. Eventually your kid will grab ahold of that sippy cup and keep on trucking. At some point, you won't remember how hard it was to get there. Now—for you—a transitional cocktail. If your cocktail repertoire heretofore has skewed toward frou-frou, super-sweet drinks, a martini reminiscent of the classic daiquiri— nothing slushy out of a whirring machine, but an elegant, hand-shaken cocktail with a long, storied history—can be just the drink to move yourself toward more mature tastes.

The Reward: *Classic Daiquir-tini*

Makes 1 martini

> 2 ounces dark rum
> 1 ounce lime juice
> About ¼ ounce simple syrup
> Splash grenadine or maraschino cherry juice
> Garnish: lime wedge or wheel

Pour all liquid ingredients into an ice-filled cocktail shaker, and shake vigorously for about 20 seconds. Strain into a chilled martini glass and add your garnish.

Classic Daiquir-tini

Water Wings on the Rocks

The Feat: *Made It Through Baby's First Swim Without Having a Nervous Breakdown*

For something so little, your baby is packed as solid as a rock. Buoyancy must be something that comes with age, because even in the bathtub your bundle of joy will sink straight to the bottom. So maybe you were a little nervous about this first swim lesson, but you were ready. Swimming-approved diapers? Check. Itty-bitty water wings? Check. Nerves of steel and a brave face for the public? Double check. So off you went with your child to the swimming pool, ready to help accomplish another first in life. Once you were there, you quickly saw that you were not the only nervous mom, and sometimes just knowing you're not alone is enough. The lesson went great, and you and your baby came through with flying colors. That look of delight on her face as she felt herself, albeit assisted by your hands, floating in the water was priceless. And the splashes and giggles that came with it were pretty awesome, too. So in honor of Baby's First Swim, your celebratory cocktail must be related to water. That's why The Blue Lagoon martini is the perfect fit. Nice, light, and a lovely shade of blue, it's the perfect cap to a swim-tastic day.

The Reward: *The Blue Lagoon*
Makes 1 martini

1 ounce vodka
1 ounce blue curaçao
Lemonade
Garnish: 1 red or green maraschino cherry (the green maraschino is usually mint-flavored)

Pour vodka and curaçao into a shaker filled with ice. Shake and strain into a martini glass. Add lemonade to fill. Garnish with the maraschino cherry of your choice.

Walk with Me Martini

The Feat: *Celebrated Baby's First Steps Without Going Overboard*

Besides those first words (which you always want to be "mama"), the most exciting first for you and your child has to be those first steps. What a joy it will be when your little one can wobble across the room toward you. You've practiced and encouraged for weeks now, and finally it happened. Tentatively at first—and then with full determination—those chubby little legs picked up one foot and then the other, making a few tiny steps forward. You cheered and clapped and laughed with your wee one at this momentous occasion. That excitement was quickly followed by the realization that once your kid learns to walk, running is not far behind. That means you'll get extra exercise as you run behind trying to keep up. But that thought is for another day, and right now you're so happy you could just skip and go naked. Luckily you thought twice about it and figured the neighbors might not take it very well, despite the good news. So instead, celebrate with the liquid version of the Skip and Go Naked martini. A little gin and beer, with a touch of sweet, makes a drink almost as light as your mood.

The Reward: *Skip and Go Naked*
Makes 1 martini

½ ounce gin
½ ounce sweet-and-sour mix
Beer to fill (lagers or pale beer recommended)

Shake the gin and sweet-and-sour mix with ice. Pour into a chilled martini glass. Fill with beer.

The Weebles Wobble Cocktail

The Feat: *Didn't Freak Out from Baby's First Fall*

Toddlers wobble a lot when they walk. In fact, they're like those old '70s toys . . . Weebles. But unlike Weebles, sometimes toddlers do fall down. When you saw your toddler take his first fall, you held your ground and did not freak out. Instead, you just wisely looked at your child as if it was no big deal, which was the right thing to do, because it kept him from freaking out! You saw that moment when you weren't sure how your kid would react. You could see the thoughts going through his mind. "Is this something I should be upset about? Mom doesn't seem to think so. Maybe it isn't?" Of course it wasn't, because toddlers are already pretty low to the ground and don't have far to fall. So congratulations! Your cooler head prevailed and saved the day. That decision helped your little one get over that little blip and get back up to walk some more. And if one good choice really deserves another, it's time for you to make up The Tailspin martini: a mix of gin and vermouth that changes its direction by adding a big splash of green Chartreuse and Campari. Just don't have too many of them—or you'll be the one ready to go into a tailspin.

The Reward: *The Tailspin*
Makes 1 martini

1½ **ounces gin**
1½ **ounces sweet vermouth**
1½ **ounces green Chartreuse**
2 **dashes Campari**
Garnish: lemon twist
Garnish: 1 cherry

Pour all liquid ingredients into a shaker with ice. Stir and strain into a martini glass. Garnish with lemon twist and cherry.

The Pacifier Peppertini

The Feat: *Broke Your Kid's Thumb Sucking/Pacifier Addiction*

Things that bring us comfort can easily become addictive habits, especially when you're a kid trying to navigate the world. For some, it's a stuffed animal or a blanket that must go everywhere. For other kids—like yours—it's sucking their thumb or needing a pacifier. Both of these things served a purpose for a time, but you know that time is past for your child, and the behavior has to stop. Now you just needed to make it happen. Well, that's easier said than done, because habits are hard to break—for anyone, let alone a kid who isn't easily swayed by what's best for oneself. You broke down and bought one of those pepper-flavored products, but quickly vetoed that option. Instead you came up with a way to reward the times your child didn't use the pacifier/thumb, and it worked! Way to go, Mom! As a reward for your positive thinking, creating positive action, you're due a cocktail. And since you didn't use any pepper on your child, why not enjoy a wonderful Peppertini?

 The Reward: *The Peppertini*
Makes 1 martini

> 3 ounces pepper vodka
> 1 ounce dry vermouth
> Garnish: 1 olive

Pour liquid ingredients into a shaker with ice. Shake and strain into a martini glass. Garnish with an olive.

The Nosey Martini

The Feat: *Retrained a Booger Eater*

At some point, every child just has to do it, even though it's one of those nasty habits we hope our kids outgrow sooner rather than later. What is it? Okay, I'll just come right out and say it . . . nose picking and booger eating! I know, it's gross, right? But today you are a *Supermom*, because you've braved the boogers, surmounted the snot, and actually redirected those gold-digging digits. Other parents will stand in awe as your little one reaches out their fingers not for their nose but for that nearby tissue. Gone are the days of worrying if your child will get a finger stuck up there, or that he might actually poke his brain. Forever in your past is being grossed out by seeing him digest that snotty salty blob. Of course, you don't actually *know* that boogers are salty . . . you just heard that somewhere, but now, it's time to celebrate your achievement in style—or at least with a little humor. What you need is a tasty concoction that recognizes your triumph while remembering to laugh at life . . . and boogers. What better than grapefruit juice blended with the perfect amount of vodka . . . served in a chilled martini glass? Oh and the humor? Add salt of course!

The Reward: *Salty Dog*

Makes 2 martinis

> 2 lime wedges and salt to rim glass
> 3 ounces vodka
> 8–10 ounces grapefruit juice
> Garnish: lime wedge

Rim chilled martini glasses with lime wedges and then dip into salt. Pour the vodka and grapefruit juice in an ice-filled shaker. Shake and pour carefully into the salt-rimmed glasses and garnish with a lime wedge.

Salty Dog

High Class Cocktail

The Feat: *Took Your Tot on His First Fancy Foray*

High tea, the ballet, a play, or the museum . . . today was the day you and your kid ventured out in your best attire and took in some culture. While you know it's important to expose your child to a variety of experiences beyond the local, wacky, Funland, you didn't know if you were pushing the envelope. Having your kid sit still is hard enough, but doing it in fancy togs . . . almost impossible. Was it too soon? Were you setting yourself up for disaster? The verdict is in, and the answer is a resounding, no, not at all! Your prep work of what to expect and what was expected on the behavior front seemed to mostly stick. And you made the right choice for your child's interests. That meant he paid attention to most of it and actually enjoyed bits and pieces throughout the experience. After a celebratory meal, you're both home and back in the comfiest clothes you own. Now, it's about you. You deserve a moment to relax and relish the fact that you and your child had quality time at a quality event. What better cocktail for this moment than the Tuxedo Martini? No fancy clothes needed.

 The Reward: *Opera Martini*

Makes 1 martini

> **2 ounces gin**
> **½ ounce Dubonnet**
> **¼ ounce maraschino liqueur**
> **1 dash orange bitters**
> **Garnish: lemon twist**

Pour ingredients, except garnish, into a shaker with ice. Stir and strain into a martini glass. Garnish with a lemon twist.

The Sweetest Words-tini

The Feat: *Didn't Cry (In Front of Your Kid) When You Heard Your First "I Love You"*

Admit it. Right after the word "Mama" you want to hear your child say, "I love you." Who wouldn't? It's the stuff that melts your heart and sears a memory into your mind. But, you've never heard it said . . . not once. And you knew if you coached or bribed your kid to say it, well it just wouldn't be the same. You were beginning to think those words would never grace your ears, and worse yet, that maybe your child wasn't saying it because he didn't love you. Then, when you least expected it, it happened. You and your kid were doing something very ordinary when that cherub-like face looked up at you and nonchalantly uttered the greatest phrase ever, "I love you, Mom." You handled it well and didn't overreact. But later, when you're alone and doing the happy parent dance, complete your reverie with this charming martini, the Angel's Lips. A delicate blend that's as smooth and sweet as the voice of your child.

The Reward: *Angel's Lips*
Makes 1 martini

| 3 ounces Benedictine |
| 1½ ounces Irish cream liqueur |

Pour ingredients in a shaker of ice. Shake gently and strain into a chilled martini glass.

Tied Up in Knots

The Feat: *Taught Your Kid to Tie Her Shoes*

By now you're pretty sure that the main reason Velcro was invented was to avoid the often tedious task of teaching your kid to tie her shoes. You can no longer count the number of times she's flopped her foot out in front of you and asked, "Will you tie my shoe?" But finally it was time for a little do-it-yourself lesson. Okay, so she didn't catch on at first. Why is it so hard to grasp something that comes so naturally to you? Well, you're showing her upside down for one thing. She watches intently and then has to flip everything upside down in her little head. Luckily you have that handy rabbit system. Making bunny ears, running around the hole, going down the hole and back up . . . it may sound funny, but it worked! Now, she's a shoe-tying genius and is off practicing with every pair of shoes in her closet. So, why not take a break with a little trip down the rabbit hole yourself? No need to call Alice, just mix and enjoy this tasty potion of a cocktail.

 ## The Reward: *Down the Rabbit Hole*
Makes 1 martini

½ **ounce carrot juice**
½ **ounce pineapple juice**
Champagne, to fill
Garnish: 1 carrot stick

Fill a shaker with ice, and then add the juices. Shake and pour into a chilled martini glass. Fill with champagne and garnish with a carrot stick.

Down the Rabbit Hole

The Balancing Act

The Feat: *Weaned Your Future Tour de France Champion off Training Wheels*

It's another rite of passage as your little one grows up . . . the removing of training wheels. From strollers to trikes to bikes, your kid has always loved being on wheels. When he first got his two-wheeler, the training wheels were great. It meant he got to ride the big boy bike! But now is the time for change. Whether he's starting to worry that he looks like a baby, or you feel that he's been leaning on them for too long, those little circles of safety have got to go. So, for the next few days your workout is running along beside your child while he rides. At first you help him get started, keep his balance, and guide him away from the mailboxes. But, pretty soon you're holding on less and less and before you know it you're just running along for moral support. Your boy is balanced and brave on just two wheels. Way to go, both of you! And now, as you sit outside and watch him ride to his heart's content, you deserve a little supportive sip for yourself. What better cocktail than the wonderful (and aptly named) Sidecar Martini?

The Reward: *Sidecar Martini*

Makes 1 martini

> 2 ounces brandy
> ½ ounce Cointreau
> 1 ounce fresh lemon juice

Combine ingredients in a shaker nearly filled with ice. Shake and strain into a martini glass.

Forbidden Martini

The Feat: *Told Your Child Where Babies Come From—Without Going Into Too Much Detail*

"Mom, where *do* babies come from?" You almost wish that your kid didn't come to you for the answer, but you don't want him hearing it from anyone else either. There's so much misinformation out there for kids on the playground and, these days, online, too. So in the big picture, you were glad the two of you talked. But in that very moment you were sweating bullets. You also had to guess a little bit at how much he really wanted to know. Ah yes, you've talked about what happens in nature, but other than that you were pretty much on your own. The most important thing isn't what you said . . . it's that you said it. Congrats on making it through an awkward chat and reminding your kid you're there for him. When he comes back with other questions, you'll stand tall again because that's how you roll. Now that you're both done squirming and he's out of the room, you deserve to celebrate rising to the challenge with the forbidden flavor of the Adam & Eve martini.

The Reward: *Adam & Eve*
Makes 1 martini

1 ounce Forbidden Fruit Liqueur
1 ounce gin
1 ounce brandy
Dash lemon juice

Pour ingredients into a shaker with ice. Shake well and strain into a martini glass.

Adam & Eve

Can You Hear Me Now–tini

The Feat: *Reluctantly Got Your Child Her First Cell Phone*

You knew the day would come, but you hoped it wouldn't be so soon. Your daughter wants a cell phone, and because she is usually off at this practice and that rehearsal, it would be safer if she always had a way to contact you. You dragged your feet a bit, but ended up getting her an affordable option. You've warned her about going over her allotted minutes and devised a plan to check in each week so she can track what she's used and what she has left. That being done, you feel pretty good about your decision. Now, every time you see her, she's chatting away with one of her girlfriends. Hey, at least it's not boys . . . yet. But what has you scratching your head is trying to figure out what she's talking about. You're not really eavesdropping; it's just that now you're hearing more of the slang words her generation uses. And, you realize it might as well be a foreign language, because you don't have a clue what they're talking about. Well, console yourself with this tequila martini, because even if you don't speak Spanish, the Habla Español Fly says, "Relax, Mom. You're doing fine."

The Reward: *Habla Español Fly*

Makes 1 martini

1½ ounces blanco tequila
1½ ounces coffee liqueur
2 ounces cold black coffee
Cream, to fill

Pour the tequila, coffee liqueur, and the cold coffee into a shaker half filled with ice. Shake and strain into a martini glass, then fill with cream. Stirring is optional.

Chapter 6
School Feats

Part of being a mom means you're involved in your child's education from day one of preschool through high school graduation. The list of support you give your kids is a long one—kind of like those school supply lists you get at the beginning of each school year. You are like a school bus getting kids to and from classes and practices and rehearsals, always making sure they have their lunch and homework. You are there for every school project, every homework question, and let's not even get started with the afterschool activities like assemblies and bake sales. And for every time your child is embarrassed by what you wore when you had carpool, you need to know your kid is equally grateful for every activity you chaperoned. No, children do not always express their gratitude . . . okay, they rarely express their gratitude . . . but trust us, it's there.

In lieu of any verbal "thank-you" or "I appreciate you" that you might not ever hear, this chapter gives you some martini recipes that may serve as a substitute. From Snickerdoodles to Sour Appletinis, you'll find cocktails for fractions, snow days, and back-to-school shopping. Hopefully they make your school year a little sweeter.

Bring Your "A" Game

The Feat: *Survived the First Day of School*

No matter how many times you go through it, the first day of school brings excitement and jitters. It happened to you when you were a kid, and now it's happening to you as a mom. The feelings are a bit different in that you're having empathy for everything your child is feeling. Maybe this year brought a change of schools, which was scary because there were so many new things: new teachers, new hallways to navigate, and new friends to make. You wondered if your child would get along, be liked, have the best teachers, and more, so both of you shared the anxious feelings of not knowing what would come. Still, you played your A game and stood tall and brave as your child mustered up the courage to go to school on day one of a new year. Things turned out okay, like you knew they would in your heart of hearts, but all that nervous energy will take a while to subside. As a part of your wind down, enjoy a cocktail that also brings its A game . . . The A-1 Martini. Now relax, it's going to be a great year.

The Reward: *A-1 Martini*

Makes 1 martini

2 ounces gin
1 ounce Grand Marnier
Splash lemon juice
Splash grenadine

Pour ingredients into a shaker with ice. Shake well and strain into a martini glass.

Conquered the Conference Cocktail

The Feat: *Aced the Year's First Parent-Teacher Conference*

Nice work, Mom. You aced the first parent-teacher conference of the year with flying colors. You were a bit nervous meeting the new teachers and hoping they thought your kid was as wonderful as you do, but no need to have worried. You did your part by showing up, participating, and letting the teachers know you were an involved, caring parent. You took note of what your child is doing well so you could congratulate him later. You also saw where there was room for improvement and where you could help. So relax and let the stress go for a bit. Take a moment to recognize all the hard work you're doing as a mom, and smile at the fact that it's being noticed. Imbibe the martini called the Ace of Spades. You earned it for acing the parent-teacher conference, so enjoy your well-deserved reward. And if you feel like dressing this cocktail up a bit, add some mint or a cherry, like the "plus" on a report card.

 The Reward: *Ace of Spades*
Makes 1 martini

> 1 ounce Crown Royal
> 1½ ounces amaretto
> Cola
> Garnish: sprig of mint

Pour Crown Royal and amaretto into an ice-filled shaker. Shake well and strain into a martini glass. Add the cola to fill. Garnish with a sprig of mint.

I've Got the Bake Sale Booze

The Feat: *Ran the Class Bake Sale*

In case you've never before been asked to manage a class bake sale (or scout troop bake sale, orchestra bake sale, etc.), here's a handy checklist of what bounties your bake-sale table should hold: dairy-free, vegan, steel-cut oatmeal, organic raisin cookies? Check. Fair-trade, antioxidant-rich, dark-chocolate, nut-free brownies? Check. Cupcakes? Check . . . Yeah, just stick with cupcakes. Nobody ever objects to cupcakes. Another thing to remember is there's a goal at the end of this sweet-fest. You're raising money for a program that your child is involved with, so put your heart into it! You will, of course, but in case any other moms forget, you can remind them. And your best friend for organizing this thing is not your best friend, it's a clipboard with a spreadsheet of who is baking what and who is manning the table when. Get everything in writing and you're good to go. Also good to go is the final bake sale item: the Snickerdoodle Martini. Okay it's not for sale, but a definite "Check." Enjoy as soon as you get home.

 ## The Reward: *Snickerdoodle Martini*

Makes 1 martini

> **Garnish: brown sugar and cinnamon rim**
> **2 ounces vanilla vodka**
> **2 ounces dark rum**
> **1 ounce hazelnut liqueur**
> **Splash simple syrup**

First, rim your martini glass with brown sugar and cinnamon and set aside. Next, combine all liquid ingredients in an ice-filled cocktail shaker. Shake vigorously for about 20 seconds, and then strain into your martini glass.

Snickerdoodle Martini

I'm Just the Help Martini

The Feat: *Didn't Do, Just Helped with, your Kid's Homework*

He did it again, waited until the last minute to finish his homework. Now you had to stay up with him to be certain it got done. Sure, it would have been a lot easier if you had sent him off to snooze-town and you did the assignment yourself. And, yes, you had done that once or twice in the past, you recalled sheepishly. But, that's not really the lesson you wanted your son to get out of this. It was more important that he learned a few things: One, there are consequences to putting off responsibilities. Two, you have to learn to rely on yourself. And three, the actual lesson the assignment is teaching. That said, you also weren't going to leave him alone at the kitchen table. So you rolled up your sleeves and coached him through it. You brainstormed ideas, helped explain a few details here and there, but let him do the actual work. When it was all done, he even thanked you! Tonight, Mom, you get an A+ and a nightcap.

The Reward: *Brainstorm*

Makes 1 martini

> 4 ounces Irish whiskey
> ½ ounce sweet vermouth
> ½ ounce Benedictine
> 2 dashes Angostura bitters

Shake all the ingredients in a martini shaker with ice, and then strain into a chilled martini glass.

The A for Effort Martini

The Feat: *Signed Off on a "No-A" Report Card*

No one is perfect, even if they're really smart and have a lot of potential. So, when your child came home with a report card that seemed to be missing a few vowels (As, that is) you didn't panic. Yes, you know she's capable of better grades. Yes, you know she spends too much time talking on the phone and not enough time doing her homework. Yet, instead of freaking out or yelling, you took a breath and counted to ten. Then all those great parental questions came pouring out of you. You know, the ones that make kids own up to their own missteps and promise to do better in the future. Good call, Mom, good call. The road to knowledge has a few dips in the road and this was just one of them. So you signed the report card and moved on to the next thing. After such a well-spoken pep talk, you need a well-deserved cocktail. How about one that blends the ideal image of education with the reality that some days aren't so sweet? Sip the lovely Sour Appletini, and know that you did a great job!

The Reward: *Sour Appletini*
Makes 1 martini

1 ounce citrus-flavored vodka
1 ounce sour apple liqueur
2 ounces sour mix

Pour all ingredients into a shaker. Shake and strain into a martini glass.

Sour Appletini

The Snow Day-tini

The Feat: *Survived a Snow Day!*

Brrr! It was cold this morning and everyone was up early. Not to get out the door on time, but to see if the weatherman was going to bring the big news of a school closure. Turned out that the snow storm was going to continue for hours, and it was officially a snow day! Wait a minute, a snow day? For you that meant rearranging schedules, not going in to work, and having your kids with you—all day. But you handled everything—from making hot chocolate and going sledding to popping popcorn and sofa snuggling—like a pro. You lived in the moment, made the best of it, and even remembered to snap a few photos. Sure you had cabin fever by the end of the day, but the promise of warmer temperatures and snow-plowed streets in the morning brought a smile to your face. With the kids all tucked in and dreaming of snowmen, it's time for you to fortify yourself with a chilly cocktail in homage to the day. The Alaska martini blends gin, Chartreuse, and orange bitters into a tasty martini that you can enjoy while wrapped in a blanket. It'll warm you up from the inside out.

The Reward: *The Alaska*

Makes 1 martini

1½ ounces gin
½ ounce yellow Chartreuse
2 dashes orange bitters
Garnish: 1 cherry

Shake the liquid ingredients in a martini shaker of ice. Strain into a martini glass. Garnish with cherry.

The Alaska

The Lovin' Lava Martini

The Feat: *Got the Science Project Volcano to Erupt!*

Okay, your kitchen looks like a disaster area, but oddly enough, that's the sign of success. There is ooh and goo all over the table and floors, and you're pretty sure there's a splotch or two on the ceiling. How can this be a good thing? Because you and your kid just created a volcano! Not just any volcano, but the fifty percent of your kid's grade, really-need-to-get-an-A science project volcano. There was more than one failed attempt, and you were about to throw in the towel and help him build a terrarium, but that would have meant a less-than-stellar project . . . followed by a less than stellar grade. Clearly, giving up was not an option for you. So it was back to the drawing board and the Internet to figure out what went awry and how to fix it. You really had a great time problem solving with your child, and better yet, you actually got the volcano to erupt. Shouts of joy filled the house, just like your fake lava filled the kitchen. Because today explosives are a good thing, you celebrate with the flavor-explosion of whiskey with anisette, a little TNT-tini. Grade: A+!

The Reward: *The TNT*

Makes 1 martini

3 ounces blended whiskey
2 ounces anisette

Pour ingredients into a shaker half filled with ice. Shake well. Strain into a martini glass.

The Broadway Bound Martini

The Feat: *Proudly Watched Your Budding Thespian Play a Tree in the School Pageant*

There are no small roles, only small actors. And so what if your kid was only a tree in the school pageant, it was the best tree ever on stage. Okay, that may be a bit over the top, but you did manage to get through the entire evening without once being embarrassed. Instead, you laughed when you should have and chuckled a bit at the countless mistakes that took place on stage. School pageants are supposed to be like that—full of silly missteps and mistakes that make your child (and all the kids) even more precious. You were rightly proud of your little Elm or Maple, or whatever tree that was supposed to be. Who knows if this will be the start of your kid's acting career, but you're going to offer encouragement every step of the way. After all, everyone has to start somewhere, right? In light of your budding Broadway Baby, make happy hour something special. Hum a few Broadway tunes, don't worry about tomorrow, and enjoy the unique and special Cabaret martini that combines gin, vermouth, and Benedictine.

The Reward: *The Cabaret*
Makes 1 martini

2 ounces gin
1½ ounces dry vermouth
½ ounce Benedictine
2 dashes bitters
Garnish: 1 cherry

Pour ingredients into a shaker with ice. Stir and strain into a martini glass. Garnish with a cherry.

If the Shoe Fits, Buy It-tini

The Feat: *Survived Back-to-School Shopping*

Is there anything more exhausting than back-to-school shopping? First there are all the clothes to buy, and matching your budget with the latest must-have fashions is never easy. With the clothes, come dress shoes, casual shoes, sports shoes, and boots . . . always boots. You haven't even had a chance to look at the school supply list your child brought home; that's another trip that will include two or three stops. And as if getting to all these stores weren't enough of a hassle, you have to drag a mostly reluctant child with you. After all, you cannot buy shoes and clothes without having them tried on first. That part might go okay, but how many kids are really excited about purchasing notebooks, pens, and pencils? And chances are that, once you think you're done, there is one other item that your child forgot to mention but has to have for some special class. *Sigh*! When you get home, kick off your shoes and enjoy the American Cobbler martini, in honor of all those shoes you just bought and the cobbler who will repair them for you.

The Reward: *American Cobbler*

Makes 1 martini

> 1½ ounces bourbon
> 1 ounce Southern Comfort
> 1–3 dashes peach brandy
> 3–5 dashes lemon juice
> Simple sugar (to taste)
> Club soda
> Garnish: peach slice
> Garnish: mint leaf

Pour the first five ingredients into an ice-filled shaker. Shake well and strain into a large martini glass. Fill with club soda. Garnish with peach slice and mint leaf.

The Overflowing Plate Cocktail

The Feat: *Said "No" to Yet Another PTA-Committee Request*

No. It's a short word, but it has a lot of power, and sometimes moms have to use it in order to stay sane. There is only so much time in any given day, and you can only do so much with it. That means it's okay to decline some of the many school-related requests that come your way. You do your part. You've chaperoned dances and coordinated bake sales, but enough is enough. That's why you said "no" to the latest request from the PTA. You probably had a twinge of guilt, and you may have even felt a little bad because you could have found a way to squeeze it into your schedule. Well, guess what? You did the right thing. You declined to step up and the world didn't end. The PTA went on to find someone else this time and you managed to keep a bit of sanity in your life. For even more sanity, have a cocktail that recognizes that you might feel bad about saying no, but celebrates how hard it can be to keep the balance. The Dirty Mother martini is a warm cocktail that's just like the hug you could use about now.

The Reward: *Dirty Mother*
Makes 1 martini

| 2 ounces brandy |
| 2 ounces coffee liqueur |

Combine the ingredients in a shaker of ice. Shake and strain into a chilled martini glass.

Super Spy Stealth Cocktail

The Feat: *Let Your Kid Walk to School Alone (Almost)*

It's hard to believe that your little boy is old enough to even think about walking to school by himself, but the years have flown by and there he was at the door. You had to let him go, because it meant so much to him—and because he really was old enough. So, making sure he had everything he needed zipped up in his backpack, you sent him out the door with a heartfelt, "Have a good day!" As soon as he got around the corner, you scuttled after him but kept out of sight. Carefully dodging behind trees and round corners, you spied on your son the entire walk to school. He did just fine and marched onto the school grounds minutes before the bell rang. You on the other hand had to get back home to nurse a few scratches because you misjudged how close you were to the neighbor's rose bush. Later on, toast your little man and raise a glass for yourself for letting him grow up. The cocktail of the hour is, of course, the Have a Good Day-tini.

The Reward: *Have a Good Day-tini*

Makes 1 martini

> 2 ounces sweet-and-sour mix
> ½ ounce vodka
> ½ ounce light rum
> ½ ounce blue curaçao
> ½ ounce gin
> Club soda

Pour the first five ingredients into a shaker half filled with ice. Shake well and strain into a chilled martini glass. Add a splash of club soda and stir gently.

I Know Something You Don't Know Cocktail

The Feat: *Showed Your Young Scholar the Difference Between an Encyclopedia and Wikipedia*

These days there is alternative music, alternative media, and even alternative lifestyles, but alternative information? Much like the way people used to believe everything they saw on television, these days the Internet seems to be the voice beyond reproach. When your child was working on a book report and shared some interesting facts that weren't quite so factual, you had to ask for the source. Unfortunately, Wikipedia was the answer to your question. Time for a life lesson for your kid, as you pulled out the old encyclopedia and shared the difference between "proven fact" and "opinion." There was initially some pushback, but that didn't slow you down. After you were able to point out some obvious misinformation, the light bulb above your child's head began to glow with understanding. So it was back to the drawing board for your child, to get some real, indisputable facts for that report. Mark one in the win column for you and head to the bar to have a toast. Mix up a favorite martini called the Alternatini, in deference to all the alternatives you face every day. Keep up the good work and enjoy your cocktail.

The Reward: *Alternatini*

Makes 1 martini

Sweetened cocoa powder	½ teaspoon sweet vermouth
3 ounces vodka	½ teaspoon dry vermouth
1 teaspoon white crème de cacao	Garnish: 1 Hershey's Kiss

Rim glass with sweetened cocoa powder. Pour remaining ingredients, except garnish, into a shaker with ice. Shake well, strain into a chilled martini glass, and garnish with a Hershey's Kiss.

The Will This Be on the Test-tini

The Feat: *Taught Your Kid How to Use Fractions*

Maybe you like math or maybe you don't, but most of the world looks upon it as a necessary evil. That said, you still had to help your child understand fractions. It can be confusing to even the brightest minds, so you had to think of a way your kid could visualize and grasp those halves and quarters. Then it hit you that money might be the answer. No you weren't going to pay him to learn, but you could use money to demonstrate fractions. Quarters were a perfect way to show, well quarters. That he understood, and you were quickly on to tenths with dimes and hundredths with pennies. His face lit up as fractions began to make sense. Before you knew it, you had a math whiz on your hands! You might even bet that he was going to ace his weekly math test, but you decided not to tell him that. There's no need for extra pressure, you just assured him he'd do fine. But why not celebrate your wisdom and teaching skills? Instead of actually betting on the outcome of his math test, just enjoy the Bet the Limit martini. It's half tequila and half Cointreau!

The Reward: *Bet the Limit*
Makes 1 martini

2 ounces tequila
2 ounces Cointreau

Pour ingredients into a shaker with ice. Stir and strain into martini glass.

No More Tears-tini

The Feat: *Got Through the Year-End Class Ceremony Without Crying*

Sometimes you can just be a blubbering mess, especially when the event has anything to do with your child. But there are times when you want to keep it together and not get all choked up and emotional. It was harder than you thought it would be, but you did it this time. You kept your emotions in check and made it through the school's year-end ceremony without crying. It's okay if you don't count the times tears welled up a bit in your eyes, because you blinked them back and kept your cool. Your child would be proud of you for not "being embarrassing." You should be proud of yourself—because you have been known to cry at sappy commercials—so controlling your teary waterfall was an act of heroic proportions. Granted, that may all be a bit over the top, but the truth is the truth. That's why when you have your next cocktail, it should be nothing but the Unsung Hero martini. It's a subtle mix of apricot and kirsch (cherry-flavored) brandies balanced out with some sweet lemonade. Make it fancy and top it with an orange slice, then promptly enjoy, because you're somebody's hero!

The Reward: *Unsung Hero*

Makes 1 martini

> 1 ounce kirsch
> 1 ounce apricot brandy
> Lemonade
> Garnish: orange slice

Pour all ingredients, except garnish, into a shaker with ice. Shake and strain into a chilled martini glass. Garnish with orange slice.

Chapter 7
Chores/ Discipline Feats

Sure, your kids go to school to learn reading, writing, and arithmetic, but you teach them most of their life lessons at home. Yes, it's an uphill battle to guide your little angels through the multitude of daily decisions it takes to live a good life. But you need to teach your child how to handle responsibility, how to treat others, and how to stay within boundaries. However, you also have to practice some discipline yourself so that your kids can learn those lessons on their own—and, of course, to embarrass your children as little as possible.

Creating chore lists, making sure your kids actually do those chores, and knowing when to say "yes" or "no" are not easy tasks—or ones that comes with any break time. So for those brief moments when you have some time to yourself and get to kick back, this chapter includes some appropriate martinis to tempt you. If you get the chance to try one of these, forget about calories and just enjoy the flavor explosions these cocktails bring.

Rock You Like a Hurricane

The Feat: *Won the Battle of the Messy Bedroom*

In the never-ending chore wars, it's Admiral Ankle Biter and his battalion of toys vs. Major Mom, who is about to experience a major meltdown. Your kid's messy bedroom really can be the bane of your existence if you let it. The best approach? Try a three-pronged attack: (1) Call in reinforcements (kid-height bookcases, bins, and other organizers to furnish a room), (2) go on the offensive, demanding that all toys either find a home off the floor or be temporarily relocated to the bed, where there'll be a . . . (3) bedspread massacre! Items still on the bed will be either given eleventh-hour reprieve or captured as POWs and exiled to basement/attic/garage/Goodwill. Don't expect perfection, just hope for cooperation. And it probably wouldn't hurt to prepare by having a great big toy box to hide stuff in before company comes. With all that flurry of activity, you need a good cocktail for keeping your cool under fire. The Hurricane Martini sounds about perfect. So shake and enjoy . . . just don't leave a mess for someone else to clean up!

The Reward: *Hurricane Martini*
Makes 1 martini

1½ ounces aged rum
1 ounce light rum
1 ounce orange juice
1 ounce passion fruit juice
½ ounce lime juice
1 dash old-fashioned bitters
Garnish: maraschino cherry or a citrus peel

Combine rums, juices, and bitters in an ice-filled shaker. Shake vigorously for about 20 seconds. Strain into a chilled martini glass. Add your garnish of choice (and perhaps a cocktail umbrella, just for fun).

Once in a Blue Moon Martini

The Feat: *Got Your Kids to Put Their Clothes in the Hamper*

Sometimes everything goes just right and things fall into place. Like when your kids' dirty clothes actually find their way into the hamper. Usually when things turn out really well, you just thank your lucky stars and move on to the next item before something changes and it all falls apart. But this time you wanted to remember everything about this turn of events in hopes of re-creating the same experience in the future. It's not that you've had a hard time getting your children to actually use the dirty clothes hamper, it's just that, well, you've never had it happen before today. So you commit to memory everything you said and how you said it, because this is a banner moment. And the kind of support, cooperation, and tidiness you experienced today felt like something wonderful, special, and rare, like a blue moon. In fact, that's why you need to commemorate this day with a cocktail that's just as unique and wonderful, like The Blue Moon martini, a light, crisp mix of gin with a bit of violet liqueur.

The Reward: *The Blue Moon*

Makes 1 martini

2 ounces gin
1 ounce violet liqueur
½ ounce fresh lemon juice
Garnish: 1 lemon twist

Shake all the liquid ingredients in a martini shaker with ice, and then strain into a chilled martini glass. Garnish with a lemon twist.

Do Your Chores Martini

The Feat: *Made the Kids Pick Their Clothes Up off the Floor*

Doing chores is never much fun, but working with someone else always makes the time go faster—at least that's what you had hoped. Certainly you'd have rather been doing something a lot more fun than picking up after your kids—something like reading a book. That's when the idea came to you. One of your favorite scenes in a book is when Tom Sawyer convinces his friends that whitewashing the fence is about the most fun a kid could have. Not wanting to miss out, his friends grab up brushes and go at it, while Tom sits back and supervises. You thought it was a brilliant approach to chores, so you took a similar tactic in getting your children to pick up their clothes off the floor. You simply turned it into a game or contest of some sort, complete with a prize. The kids quickly pushed you aside and grabbed up dirty socks as if their lives depended on it, which gave you time to think of a worthy reward for the winner. While pondering your prize, why not salute Tom Sawyer and all his friends by creating this wonderful, slightly sweet gin cocktail, the Huckleberry Finn Gin Martini?

The Reward: *Huckleberry Finn Gin Martini*
Makes 1 martini

> **3 ounces huckleberry-infused Jenever (Dutch gin)**
> **Garnish: huckleberry bloom**

Shake the huckleberry Jenever in a martini shaker of ice and strain into a martini glass. Garnish with a huckleberry bloom.

The Bargaining Chip Cocktail

The Feat: *Renegotiated Your Kid's Allowance*

Union negotiations are probably not as hard as talking with your kid about allowance. Your kid wanted more, of course, but you were on a budget and only had so much wiggle room. Back and forth you went about what would be done to earn the allowance and how often it would be paid. Your child lamented the fact that, "All the other kids get more," but this didn't actually hold sway with you—and your child's argument even lost a little steam when you restated the fact that there didn't have to be any allowance at all. It wasn't that you didn't want your kid to have an allowance, but there was a limit to what you felt was appropriate. It's okay to stand firm. You know that your child will always take as much as you'll give, so you set a limit. Finally, your kid agreed, not only to the amount, but that the amount was fair. Now, mix yourself up a silly martini called the Cookie Monster. It's a sweet treat that will make you remember that, like the Cookie Monster, your child will always want more . . .

 ## The Reward: *Cookie Monster*
Makes 1 martini

| 1 ounce Maui Blue Hawaiian Schnapps |
| Pineapple juice |

Shake schnapps in a martini shaker with ice, then strain into a chilled martini glass, and add pineapple juice to fill.

Because I Said So-tini

The Feat: *Said "No," Meant It, and Followed Through*

"*No*" means "no" in any language (no, nope, nein, nah, nee . . . you get the idea). But the important thing is this time you meant it! And not only did you mean it, you stuck to your guns. Yes, it was hard when your little angel's bottom lip started to quiver and the tears rolled down those chubby cheeks. It got even tougher when tears turned to anger. "It's not fair," you heard, followed by stomping down the hall and slamming of the bedroom door. It isn't fair, right? Why do moms have to be the bad guy? Oh wait . . . you're setting boundaries, teaching life lessons, and making the decision that's truly best for your little one. So you shored yourself up, walked down the hall, and knocked on that closed door. Sitting on the bed, you gave one of the best parents-know-best speeches ever! And, it worked! Tears were dried, a priceless hug was shared, and perhaps begrudgingly, your word and will stood firm. Whew! Now, it's time to pat yourself on the back. You deserve to enjoy the bittersweet victory of parental success with the ideal bittersweet cocktail—the Negroni Martini. It's a little gin, a little Campari, and a little sweet vermouth to smooth out the rough edges. Nice!

The Reward: *Negroni Martini*
Makes 1 martini

1½ ounces gin
1½ ounces sweet vermouth
1½ ounces Campari
Garnish: lemon twist

Pour liquid ingredients into a shaker with ice. Stir and strain into a martini glass. Garnish with lemon twist.

Negroni Martini

The TV Land-tini

The Feat: *Set a Television Schedule*

Television is a wonderful invention that can be both educational and entertaining. However, when it becomes the sole activity for anyone, especially young people, sometimes you just have to pull the plug. And that's just what you did when you saw that your kids were going to spend yet another afternoon glued to the "idiot box." You put your foot down and put up a television watching schedule. You let your kids know that channel surfing was going to be balanced with homework, chores, and playing outside. At first there were moans and groans of unfairness, but you held firm, despite the temptation to give in and return the remote. You assure them you don't hate television. You even share a few of your favorite shows that you watched on TV Land when you were younger, including *I Dream of Jeannie*. Good for you, Mom, because you know limiting TV time is the best thing to do, and you know your kids will eventually get used to the new rules. Now, with the kids off playing or doing homework, you wax a bit nostalgic and enjoy a cocktail that raises its glass to classic television . . . the I Dream of Genie Martini, complete with a poof of smoke!

The Reward: *I Dream of Genie Martini*

Makes 1 martini

> 2 ounces cherry-flavored vodka
> 3 ounces pink lemonade
> Splash grenadine for color
> Large cube of food-grade dry ice

Shake the first three ingredients in a martini shaker of ice. Strain into a martini glass. Using tongs, drop in a large cube of food-grade dry ice to activate your Genie Martini. Be extremely cautious—do not touch or drink the ice. Use a cocktail straw in your martini glass as a safety precaution.

Victory Is Yours Martini

The Feat: *Got Out of the Store Without Buying Your Child a Good-Behavior Bribe*

It's the little things in life that often mean the most, especially to moms running around doing errands with their kids in tow. Everything takes a bit longer, and almost without fail, kids end up misbehaving on some level. The forms bad behavior can take come in many shapes and sizes . . . too many to list. But, the foolproof solution that works for most moms is to offer a toy or treat to bribe them into acting right. It's something you don't like to do, and every outing brings the hope that either your child will behave or that you won't acquiesce to the old pattern. That's why you vowed this day would be different. Expectations were set before you left the house, and you were clear there would be some accountability involved. Let's hope you recorded that speech, because something you said worked. You made it through a list of errands as long as your arm, without so much as a peep of bad manners or surly answers. Take that victory lap around the parking lot and give credit where credit is due. This win should be toasted with a Victory Collins Martini, a drink as refreshing as a well-behaved child.

The Reward: *Victory Collins Martini*

Makes 2 martinis

1½ ounces vodka
3 ounces lemon juice
3 ounces grape juice (unsweetened)
1 teaspoon powdered sugar
Garnish: 2 orange slices

Pour all ingredients, except garnish, into a shaker with ice. Shake and strain into chilled martini glasses. Garnish with orange slices.

Victory Collins Martini

The Good Housekeeping Martini

The Feat: *Sported an Immaculate House for the Neighborhood Meeting*

You work hard to keep your house neat and tidy, but with kids and everything else on your plate, it can sometimes be an uphill battle. Even though your house is usually in pretty good shape, there always seems to be a stack of laundry that needs attention or a counter that needs to be wiped. But the neighborhood meeting was held at your house this time so the pressure was on full steam. You know you shouldn't be worried about what other people think, but the idea of being judged by some of the community moms left you a bit nervous. Your kids pitched in and you all vacuumed, dusted, mopped, and shined every inch of the house from top to bottom. Everything looked beautiful, if you did say so yourself. The meeting was held and you received lots of positive comments on your home. It made you feel proud because getting it in shape had been a family project, and you were sure to thank your kids for pitching in to help. All's now quiet on the western front, and it's time for you to unwind with a simple yet elegant cocktail . . . the Beautiful. Enough said.

 The Reward: *Beautiful*

Makes 1 martini

2 ounces cognac
2 ounces Grand Marnier

Pour ingredients into a martini glass and serve.

Do What's Right-tini

The Feat: *Brokered Peace Between the Kids at the Playground*

There are a few constants on the playground. One of them is a swing set, and the other one is a bully. No matter the circumstances, no matter the neighborhood, there always seems to be one kid who makes it his job to push around other kids. It's best when kids can work through these things themselves, but every once in a while a grown-up needs to step in and guide the way. That's just what you did when you saw a disagreement that was well on its way to becoming a fight. It's much easier to settle an argument than to stop a fight, so you took action. The great thing is you didn't tell the children what to do. You acted more like a mediator as you taught the kids how to communicate and settle their differences. Once things started to calm down, you stepped away, and as kids will often do, they made peace among themselves. Sure, the bully will probably still do his thing again, but today ended on a better note. When you get home, warm yourself up with the knowledge you did the right thing and a warm cocktail called the Piston Bully . . . it's the right thing, too.

The Reward: *Piston Bully*

Makes 1 martini

---

3 ounces hot black coffee
½ ounce Kahlúa
½ ounce Grand Marnier
Garnish: whipped cream

Carefully pour liquid ingredients into a room-temperature, or warmed, martini glass. Top with whipped cream.

Make Me Proud Martini

The Feat: *Watched Proudly as Your Kid Stood Up for a Friend in Need*

This may come as a surprise to you, but how your child acts at home isn't always a reflection of how she behaves in public. You've always taught your kid right from wrong, and you hoped you were a good example of how she should treat others. But you didn't know if your lessons took until the other day. We've all experienced peer pressure and know how hard it can be to stand up to that, especially when you're standing up for someone else. But your daughter was amazing. There was a group of kids mistreating one of your daughter's friends. Before you could even think about what to do, she stepped up and made it clear that it was not right to treat her friend that way. Their behavior was, as she said, not cool. Wow! That was your kid doing the right thing without any prompting. Hmmm . . . wonder where she learned that? Be proud, Mom, because that is what good parenting is all about. In fact, when you're ready for your next cocktail, relive that moment by mixing up the wonderfully named Playmate martini. Bask in the fact that you've turned your daughter into a friend that a kid would like to have.

The Reward: *Playmate*
Makes 1 martini

½ **ounce apricot brandy**
½ **ounce brandy**
½ **ounce Grand Marnier**
½ **ounce orange juice**
1 egg white
Dash bitters

Pour ingredients into a shaker with ice. Shake and strain into a martini glass.

Playmate

The Bite Your Tongue-tini

The Feat: *Refrained from Yelling at Your Kid's Soccer Coach from the Sidelines*

Sometimes it's just hard to keep your mouth shut. Still, you never want to be one of *those* parents at your kid's soccer game. You know, the ones who end up on YouTube videos being lambasted all over the Internet for un-sportsman-like behavior. Plus, it would completely embarrass your child and that's not what you're going for here. But a bad call is a bad call, and someone needs to talk to the coach, right? Well, maybe that person isn't you, and it's certainly not you when you're so upset. So you bite your tongue and count to ten, or twenty, or whatever it takes. After all, you're not the coach, and you know you wouldn't even want to take on the job. Maybe the whole thing won't seem like such a big deal the next day. You decide to just watch the rest of the game and mind your manners. And when you talked with your kid on the way home, he told you he was glad you didn't overreact like some of the other parents. See? That was a good call, Mom. So, in honor of *not* getting in trouble and needing a time out, why not sip on a Time Out martini?

 The Reward: *Time Out*

Makes 1 martini

Sugar
3 ounces Jägermeister
1 ounce anisette

Rim martini glass with sugar. Pour ingredients into a shaker with ice. Shake well and strain into glass.

Overprotective Is Overrated Martini

The Feat: *Watched Your Little Guy Square Off in the Wrestling Ring Without Jumping In to Save Him*

Do you ever wonder if kids realize how often parents restrain themselves from doing things that pop into their heads? Seriously, the fact that something would embarrass your son really does factor into more decisions than he realizes. A perfect example is when you decided to stay in your seat instead of rushing into the wrestling ring to save your boy from being hurt. You knew that other kid was a lot bigger and stronger, but you knew your son had to fight his own battles, especially on the wrestling team. Good call, Mom! You pulled yourself together, watched the match with one hand over your eyes, and stayed in your seat. That took discipline. That took strength. That took you envisioning the entire incident with you in the ring and realizing it was just a bad idea. You earned some serious good karma points, even if your son has no idea what you went through. How about some liquid mojo to keep you going? Shake up the Good Karma martini and enjoy the raspberry/melon goodness, while you reflect on yet one more battle you've won without being overprotective.

 The Reward: *Good Karma*

Makes 1 martini

> 1 ounce raspberry liqueur
> 1 ounce melon liqueur
> 1 ounce pineapple juice
> 1 ounce sweet-and-sour mix

Pour all ingredients into a martini shaker of ice and shake. Strain into a martini glass.

The Excusez-Moi-tini

The Feat: *Endured a Run-In with a Parenting Snob*

Who knows what sets these snobs off? It could be the kind of stroller you push, the hold you elect to use for burping your baby, or the fact that you've yet to teach your infant how to sign words like "milk" and "Harvard." Inevitably, out in public, you will feel the white-hot scorn of another parent's judgmental gaze, often precipitating a rash of inadequacy and resentment that rushes across your neck, cheeks, and forehead. You just started this parenting gig, and already you're being ambushed with unexpected performance reviews. Stop. Do not let this person bug you. Be the mature one by remembering this mantra of adulthood: I'm rubber, you're glue. Then put a pin in all those sour feelings until you're able to go home and fix yourself a French Martini, the sweet antidote to snideness.

The Reward: *French Martini*

Makes 1 martini

> 2 ounces vodka
> ¾ ounce raspberry liqueur
> 1 ounce pineapple juice
> Garnish: pineapple wedge

Combine your vodka, liqueur, and juice in an ice-filled cocktail shaker. Shake vigorously for about 20 seconds. Strain into a chilled martini glass and garnish with pineapple wedge.

Call It a Comeback

The Feat: *Snapped Back at a Parenting Snob*

Some might not call issuing a tart-tongued retort to the stranger who said something snippy about your child's momentarily less-than-perfect behavior a feat. In fact, some might see it as a fault, so make sure you use just the right words. The following statements have been real-life-mother-approved as ones that toe the line between politeness and prudence. Here's your arsenal of one-liners for when the time comes:

"Thank you for your unsolicited parenting advice."

"We don't do what works best for you. We do what works best for us."

"Well, at least it's only one of my kids who's screaming/running around/etc." (Effective in a particularly bizarre way when you've only got one child.)

"I'll take that into consideration." (Then slowly wander away with a blank look on your face.)

Once you've put that parenting snob in her place, head home and reward your quick-wittedness with The Witty Comeback martini.

 ## The Reward: *The Witty Comeback*
Makes 1 martini

2 ounces rye whiskey
½ ounce lemon juice
½ ounce Averna Amaro Siciliano (an Italian liqueur)
½ ounce ginger syrup
Garnish: orange peel

Combine whiskey, lemon juice, Averna, and ginger syrup in an ice-filled cocktail shaker, and shake vigorously for about 20 seconds. Strain into a chilled martini glass and garnish with orange peel.

Chapter 8

Mom-Specific Feats

It all starts when you bring that sweet little bundle of joy home for the first time. As a mom, you are on a journey that will stretch you to the limits, show you how strong you are, and bring you breathtaking moments of joy and heartache that you will remember forever. You will question yourself and cheer yourself, sometimes in the same day. Your will wear many, many hats without question and be the rock that holds your family together. In other words, Mom, you are amazing, awesome, and wonderful.

This chapter will help you celebrate every moment, especially those rare occasions when you get some "me time" without the kids. Yes, you love your children, but you also need to relax, recharge, and do some things that are just about you. So the following martinis are just for these circumstances. They are a pat on the back, a nerve soother, a celebration, and a comforter. From giving birth and giving back to taking charge and kicking butt, you are what your kids will want to be when they grow up.

Stir It, Don't Shake It, Because It Took Nine Months to Make It

The Feat: *Had a Baby!*

Congratulations are definitely in order! You just accomplished one of the most amazing feats possible . . . you had a baby! You now have a pure, precious, untarnished, immaculate, and sublime little newborn. And, whether you are imbibing yet, or just letting friends and family raise a glass, the perfect celebratory cocktail is the martini, also pure, precious, untarnished, immaculate, and sublime. Another way a baby is like a martini: People obsess over how "wet" or "dry" theirs is. In confusing cocktail nomenclature, the less *dry vermouth* a martini contains, the drier that martini is considered. This recipe's ratio is tuned to modern tastes, veering toward extra dry—which is exactly what you want your newborn's diaper to be. But, as with any parenting survival measure, experiment to find what suits you best.

The Reward: *Classic Gin Martini*

Makes 1 martini

2½ ounces dry gin
¼ ounce dry vermouth
Garnish: green olive or a lemon twist

Pour your gin and vermouth into an ice-filled mixing glass. Stir briskly for about a minute. Strain into a chilled martini glass and add preferred garnish.

Classic Gin Martini

The One-Handed Zen Master-tini

The Feat: *Learned to Type/Text/Eat/Knit/Do Your Makeup One-Handed (While the Other Holds the Baby)*

Who knew you could become ambidextrous when you had a child? Seriously, necessity has made you adept at doing all things with one hand, because the other hand is always busy holding your baby. Okay, so that's not the exact definition of "ambidextrous," but you definitely are more coordinated than you used to be. With one hand, you can type, text, eat, tie your shoes, put on your makeup, and sew on a button! Well, maybe not the button thing, but it's almost like that. Your life has become a physical balancing act that's practically Zen like. You are at one with your baby on your hip and have embraced the yin and yang of moving through life as such. If you ever get a chance to put your child down (those rare and precious nap times, perhaps), you need to raise a glass to your heightened coordination. Try the Woo Woo-tini, also a balancing act. It's equal parts vodka and peach schnapps, topped with crisp cranberry juice. Bet you could even make it with one hand tied behind your back.

The Reward: Woo Woo-tini

Makes 1 martini

1 ounce vodka
1 ounce peach schnapps
Cranberry juice, to fill

Pour the vodka and peach schnapps into a martini shaker half filled with ice. Shake well and strain into a chilled martini glass. Fill with cranberry juice.

The Family Feud Martini

The Feat: *Survived a Visit from the Family*

You love family, you really do. However, you can only handle them for so long before they start pushing every button you have. You learned something over the past few days, though. You learned that a family visit after you've had a child is very different from your prekid visits. Now that you have kids, your family packs extra, unsolicited parenting advice in their luggage. Of course, you know everyone really meant well, but after a few days, all that insight was exhausting. Never mind though, because you survived. You made it through all the craziness and all the love. Yes love, because even with all those buttons pushed, now that they're gone, you miss them just a little. No worries, you know they'll come again, and until then you have time to recover. So plop down on the couch, and start your recovery with a drink that's all about family. The Family. Enjoy The Godfather. It's a drink you can't refuse.

The Reward: *The Godfather*

Makes 1 martini

> **4 ounces blended Scotch whiskey**
> **1½ ounces amaretto**

Pour Scotch and amaretto into a martini shaker half filled with ice. Shake well and strain into a martini glass.

You Matter Martini

The Feat: *Proved Yourself Culturally Relevant to Your Kid*

You actually made your kid take notice of something you knew, that she didn't. Not just anything, but something your child was actually interested in. That, of course, meant pop culture, but pop culture was better than no culture at all. Maybe it's not earth shattering to know all the films Johnny Depp was in *before* he became Captain Jack Sparrow, but since your little one didn't know he had made *any* films before hitting the high seas, it was kind of cool. You were like a movie star savant, and your daughter looked up to you as if you were actually relevant. Enjoy the moment, because with kids, you never know how long it might last. No worries though. You know that the mother/child relationship has many ups and downs, much like a ship being tossed around in a stormy sea. So, hoist your sails and hang on for the ride. And to help you get through some of the down times, sip on—what else, but—the Pirate's Sour martini. As you dive in, the cinnamon sweet top gets balanced out with sour mix and bitters. Both sweet and bitter, like a good drink, and a good life, should have. Ahoy, matey!

The Reward: *Pirate's Sour*
Makes 1 martini

2 ounces dry gin
1½ ounces sour mix
3 dashes Angostura bitters
Float of Goldschläger

Shake the first three ingredients in a martini shaker with ice. Strain into a martini glass, and float the Goldschläger on top.

Anything You Can Do, That Would Be Great, Because I Could Do with a Cocktail

The Feat: *Learned to Share the Load*

Look up "for better or worse" in the dictionary and you'll find a picture of a screaming baby in a crib and two new parents staring at one another, dumbstruck. Your little one may have been your singular burden to bear for nine body-battering months, but now she's a shared responsibility, equal parts "yours, mine, and ours." And the truth is your partner is your only true ally in this whole parenting thing. Especially once the fanfare from family and friends dies down, and it's just the three of you left to your own devices, wondering what the heck is supposed to happen next. Here's a hint: Talk it out. Listen and learn. Ask what your partner thinks. Sometimes father really does know best. (Really!)

The Reward: *Fifty-Fifty Martini*

Makes 1 martini

2 ounces dry gin
2 ounces dry vermouth (equal to the amount of gin you decide to use)
Garnish: cocktail olive

Pour gin and vermouth into an ice-filled mixing glass and stir briskly for about a minute. Strain into a chilled martini glass and add garnish.

You're Sexy and You Know It-tini

The Feat: *Brought Sexy Back*

You feel good about you, and that's great. In fact, you feel more than good, you feel sexy, and that's awesome! What makes you feel sexy is up to you and no one can take that away. It could be on the outside like getting a new haircut or fitting back into your skinny jeans. It could also be something on the inside, like achieving a goal or gaining self-confidence. But as a busy mom you sometimes misplace your "sexy," and that's why bringing your sexy back, in whatever form works for you, is a feat worth shouting about! Promise to use your sensual powers only for good, but promise to use them all the same. Whether it's working a new sexy strut or playing around with your hubby in the bedroom, own it and have fun. In fact, why not celebrate yourself with a classic sexy cocktail? Shake up the Between the Sheets martini, and dance around the kitchen. While you're at it, roll back the rug, crank up the music, put on those vampy pumps, and party down. Enjoy this cocktail alone or share it with someone special, it's all about whatever your heart desires!

The Reward: *Between the Sheets*
Makes 1 martini

¾ **ounce light rum**
¾ **ounce brandy**
¾ **ounce triple sec**
½ **ounce lemon juice**
Garnish: 1 lemon twist

Pour all liquid ingredients into a martini shaker half filled with ice. Shake well and strain into a chilled martini glass. Garnish with a lemon twist.

Working Nine to Five Martini

The Feat: *Went Back to Work*

At some point, many moms have to return to work, and the list of reasons for returning to the nine-to-five world can be as long as a mom's daily to-do list. But, from enjoying some time outside of the house to missing the extra time with your kid, it can be a rough transition. And that doesn't include the stress and worry of getting back into the work groove and getting up to speed on whatever your job entails. Emotions and responsibilities are coming from all directions. It's no wonder that so many moms are sometimes ready for the clock to read 5 P.M. You deserve some extra praise because you now have two jobs. So salute yourself and the role you play in your family's life with the sweet, rich reward called the After Five martini. The creamy, coffee, peppermint flavors will ease away the worries of the day. Just take a moment and stop the clock. This is mom time!

The Reward: *After Five*

Makes 1 martini

> 1½ ounces Irish cream liqueur
> 1½ ounces Kahlúa
> 1½ ounces peppermint schnapps

Pour all ingredients into an ice-filled shaker. Shake well and strain into a martini glass.

Mid-Morning Martini

The Feat: *Went Out to Brunch*

Hey, remember brunch? That thing you used to do before you had kids and after you spent your Saturday and Sunday mornings sleeping in? Back then it was just part of your week's natural rhythm: Work hard Monday through Friday, then sleep-brunch-nap-dinner Saturdays and Sundays. Little did you realize how much you'd one day come to miss those soggy eggs Benedict, not to mention brunch's classic cocktail accompaniment, the Champagne Fizz. Once you had kids, you may have thought that you'd never be able to enjoy a proper brunch again. And yet here you are, gossipy tongue at the ready, girlfriends around the table, ready to get down to the business of brunch—which is, blessedly, the business of doing nothing at all.

The Reward: *Champagne Fizz*
Makes 1 martini

2 ounces gin
1 ounce lemon juice
1 teaspoon sugar
Chilled champagne, to fill

Combine gin, lemon juice, and sugar in a shaker half filled with ice and shake. Strain into a chilled martini glass. Fill with champagne.

It's Your Time Martini

The Feat: *Actually Made It to a Girls' Night Out*

You can't remember the last time you had quality girlfriend time, but you knew it was time to make some time for your friends when the only songs that played in your head were nursery rhymes, and the last book you read had more pictures than words. Of course you love your children, but you also need to love yourself a little. So no last-minute cancellations . . . not this time . . . not tonight. You put on your best "non-mom-jeans," topped them with something shiny, slipped into some not-so-sensible shoes, and hit the road—or the dance floor. It didn't really matter what you did. You were just out with some grown-up girlfriends having a blast. Laughing, talking, sharing, and supporting, you were all there for each other. It was just what the doctor ordered to pep you up and keep you going. Another thing to pep you up is a nice grown-up beverage. Since you're feeling all sassy and sexy, it's got to be time for the classic girls' night out cocktail—the Cosmopolitan.

 ## The Reward: *Cosmopolitan*
Makes 1 martini

> 2 ounces vodka
> 1 ounce triple sec
> 1 ounce cranberry juice
> ½ ounce lime juice

Pour all ingredients into a shaker half filled with ice. Shake well. Strain into a martini glass. Note: To upgrade this popular drink, use a premium vodka and Cointreau in place of the triple sec. Flavored vodkas can be used to vary the taste.

Cosmopolitan

The Makeover Martini

The Feat: *Went for a Mama Makeover*

Maybe your sense of fashion has been a little bit skewed lately. Sometimes as a mom, your idea of getting dressed up means there are no stains on your clothes and your hair is in a ponytail instead of flying out in all directions. What happened to the gal who refused to walk out of the house until she was perfectly coifed? Well, one of the biggest sacrifices moms make is taking care of themselves. A day that includes a shower is now considered a good day. But hold the phone! Taking time for yourself is vital because you, amazing Mom, matter. Finally, you put yourself first and headed out to the spa for a makeover. No guilt allowed; you farmed your child out to a babysitter, because it was pampering time! Whether you got your hair done, or a skin treatment, or a mani-pedi . . . or hopefully all of the above . . . it was really about taking a moment and letting others do for you. Plus, you felt great at the end of it all. Why not extend that bit of bliss at home and shake up the Seventh Heaven martini? A little gin, juice, and mint . . . it's a real slice of heaven for your mouth.

The Reward: *Seventh Heaven*

Makes 1 martini

> 3½ ounces gin
> 1 ounce maraschino liqueur
> ½ ounce fresh grapefruit juice
> Garnish: 1 sprig of mint

Shake all the liquid ingredients in a martini shaker with ice, and then strain into a chilled martini glass. Garnish with sprig of mint.

Skinny Jean Gin-tini

The Feat: *Fit Into Your Skinny Jeans Again!*

Woo hoo! You did it; you're back into your skinny jeans and feeling good! While it's not about the number on the scale, or even the size of the jeans, being at your best is just awesome. Whether it was lingering baby weight or extra pounds from the holidays, those pounds didn't belong to you, and it was time to give them up. More exercise, fewer carbs, more veggies, less sugar, whatever you did, it worked! You stuck with it through all kinds of temptations and plateaus and have emerged the victor. Now that you're back into those delicious denims, the last thing you want is to undo what you've done. But, that doesn't mean you can't celebrate and raise a glass of cheer. There are calorie-conscious cocktails at your fingertips. Forget the fancy (and pricey) premixed beverages. Why not reward yourself with a thin little something you can make and enjoy without leaving the house? Shake and pour the Thin Gin-tini and revel all you want, guilt free.

The Reward: *Thin Gin-tini*
Makes 1 martini

| 2 ounces dry gin |
| Diet ginger ale, to fill |

Pour gin into an ice-filled shaker. Shake and strain into a martini glass. Fill with diet ginger ale.

Life Is But a Dream-tini

The Feat: *Managed to Get the House All to Yourself*

Shhh. What's that? Do you hear it? That's silence, Mom. Isn't it wonderful? You actually had the house to yourself for an afternoon and it was so quiet you didn't even recognize the sound . . . or lack thereof. These experiences are rare for busy moms, but when they do happen, it's a dream come true. Of course you love your family, but having a bit of quiet time in your own house isn't such a bad option either. What you do with this time is completely up to you, but any sort of chores are highly discouraged. Forget about sorting the sock drawer or organizing the pantry for today. Your list of options is best when it includes things like taking a bubble bath, reading a book, having a nap, or watching a chick flick. Eat whatever you want, because no one is around to tell on you. The other thing you need to enjoy is a nice cocktail in honor of your newfound solace. Just its name—The Dreamsicle Martini—seems like an ideal homage to you being home alone. But wait until you taste the decadent mix of Irish cream liqueur and orange juice. It's, well, dreamy!

The Reward: *The Dreamsicle Martini*
Makes 1 martini

1½ ounces Irish cream liqueur
3½ ounces orange juice

Pour ingredients into a shaker half filled with ice. Shake and strain into a martini glass.

The Mom Meltdown Martini

The Feat: *Survived a Mom Meltdown*

It was bound to happen, because a person can only go so long before they just have to let it all out. You have the most important job in the world, raising a child—and the pressure of wanting to do everything right, the fear you're doing it all wrong, the lack of sleep, and the endless to-do list is enough to make anyone go a little crazy. The important thing about having a mom meltdown is to do it without guilt and then move on down the road—and that's what you did. Sure, you hit your boiling point, and yes, there were lots of tears. But even if you screamed like a banshee, it's okay. You felt a lot better after it was all over, and you got through it without anyone getting hurt, so all is well. Now, before you start worrying about that to-do list, take another moment to relish your meltdown. Pull out the ingredients for a yummy cocktail, and enjoy The Banshee martini!

The Reward: *The Banshee*
Makes 1 martini

1 ounce banana liqueur
1 ounce white crème de cacao
2 ounces cream

Combine ingredients in a martini shaker of ice. Shake, and then pour into a martini glass.

The We Did It Again Cocktail

The Feat: *Had Your Second (or Third or Fourth) Child*

Passing out cigars may be passé, but celebrating the birth of a child never goes out of style. While you had a much better idea what you were getting into and going to go through this second (or third or fourth) time around, that does not make it easier. So let's hear it for you, Mom! We all give kudos to you for carrying that sweet bundle of joy for nine months, and for enduring all those things that happen to your body (and brain) when you're pregnant—and afterwards! The great thing is you already know about the sleepless nights, and hopefully, you still have a crib and the other basics on hand. So while the job of motherhood is still ahead of you, you've got some great experience to take along for the ride. Another thing to take along for the ride is a nice tasty cocktail, as long as you're not the one driving (or breastfeeding), that is. This classic gin-based cocktail is fresh with orangy citrus and just the right amount of sweet. And like the latest addition to your family, it's hard not to love. Congratulations and enjoy!

 The Reward: *Stork Club Martini*

Makes 1 martini

> 1½ ounces gin
> ½ ounce Cointreau
> ¼ ounce fresh lime juice
> 1 ounce fresh orange juice
> Dash Angostura bitters
> Garnish: 1 orange twist

Shake all liquid ingredients with ice. Strain into a martini glass. Garnish with an orange twist.

Stork Club Martini

At One with Mom Martini

The Feat: *Achieved Zen State of Calm*

As a mom, your world is often frantic, chaotic, and loud (very loud). You keep going from one thing to another, doing your best to keep it all together. Sometimes all you want, or crave, is a moment or two of silence where you can actually hear yourself think. In that moment you imagine you will find calm. A Zen state of calm. What a dream-like feeling that would be, right? Yet every time you thought you were close, something came along and disrupted the quiet. From a phone call to a child's shout, something or someone kept demanding your atten-tion. Not so this time. Today, you found a bubble of nirvana where your nerves were soothed and your mind was peaceful. You owned the cool, calm, and collected atmosphere surrounding you. That serene setting deserves to be sealed with a drink. A nice, tranquil cocktail that holds the power to keep you composed. Enter, the Wonderland Green Mint Teani. Sweetened with simple syrup and kicked up a notch with light rum, this warm beverage is sure to help you keep your cool. Remember it anytime you need to reclaim your Zen.

The Reward: *Wonderland Green Mint Teani*
Makes 1 martini

5 mint leaves
½ ounce simple syrup
2 lime wedges
1 ounce light rum
Hot green tea, to fill
1 tablespoon honey, or to taste

Muddle the mint in simple syrup with the lime wedges. Add the rum. Pour into a room-temperature or warmed martini glass and top with steaming green tea. Sweeten with honey to taste.

Wonderland Green Mint Teani

The Nick of Time-tini

The Feat: *Dashed Out of Work, Made the Recital Just in Time*

It was one of those days where everything and everyone was behind schedule. From morning traffic, to the first meeting of the day being delayed, to the long line at the lunch counter, you were fighting the clock every step of the way. Why today? Of all days, this was one where you could not stay late. It was your child's first recital and there was no way you were going to miss even a second of the show. Maybe it was just Murphy's Law that kept you one step behind all day, but finally, after a day spent moving at breakneck speed, you wrapped up your day at the very last minute. You dashed to the car and headed across town hoping traffic would not be a repeat of the morning crush. With just minutes to spare, you parked your car and ran into the auditorium, getting settled just as the lights went down. Whew! After the backstage flowers and at-home good nights, sit back, put your feet up, and relax. To help you unwind, sip on the wonderful Ankle Breaker martini, and be glad you didn't break yours in all the rush to get to the show on time.

The Reward: Ankle Breaker

Makes 1 martini

2 ounces 151 proof rum
1 ounce cherry brandy
1 ounce lime juice
1 teaspoon simple syrup

Pour all ingredients into a shaker with ice. Shake and strain into a chilled martini glass.

All Booked Up Martini

The Feat: *Managed a Mega Carpool Schedule*

Whether it's the start of the school term or the beginning of a brand-new year, when you have kids, you have carpools. Getting that schedule sorted out can be a real bear when you factor in before- and afterschool activities, your work schedule, travel, and more. This year it was your turn to get things down on paper—and more importantly—approved and okayed by all the participating parents. After countless drafts, calls, and e-mails, you did it! You have a completed mega carpool schedule, and it's been sent out to everyone. Nice work, Mom! Of course, you know there'll be changes, and it will feel as though you're doing more than your fair share of driving, but that's the way everyone feels. Still, you've wondered about slapping a magnetic taxi cab sign on the side of the car just for fun. Maybe you could get one of those meters, too? If nothing else, it might make you smile a little more as you wait for passengers. But if you want to smile right now, whip up the Tijuana Taxi martini and take the scenic route!

The Reward: *Tijuana Taxi*
Makes 1 martini

1 ounce gold tequila
½ ounce blue curaçao
½ ounce passion fruit liqueur
2 ounces lemon-lime soda
Garnish: orange slice
Garnish: 1 cherry

Pour liquors into a martini shaker half filled with ice. Shake and pour into a chilled martini glass. Add lemon-lime soda to fill. Garnish with an orange slice and a cherry.

Chapter 9

Out-and-About Feats

Someone, at some point, must have done a real study about the amount of time moms spend in their minivans and SUVs toting family back and forth, but for now let's just say it's a boatload of time! You handle everyday trips to schools, grocery stores, and doctors' appointments as if that kind of scheduling was second nature. But you also handle road trips and vacations (not always the same thing) with the panache of a travel agent—one who always remembers the snacks and packs the must-have blankets and stuffed animals.

You should definitely get frequent flyer miles or some other kind of cool reward for always getting your kids to and fro. That's why this chapter has a list of out-and-about martinis for your drinking enjoyment. Of course, it goes without saying that none of these cocktails should be enjoyed while you're doing the actual driving. But once that van or car is parked at home and the keys are on the counter, feel free to belly up to the bar and have an adult beverage. A classy Vesper or a decadent S'moretini could be just what you need to end your day in style.

The Brave New World Martini

The Feat: *Ventured Into Public with a Newborn*

There are so many things to think (and worry) about when you take your little one out into the world for the first time. More than likely it was just a quick trip to the doctor's office for that newborn checkup, but it still makes most moms nervous. You were no exception as you bundled and wrapped your wee one. First, you had to pack the diaper bag, which had to be packed with all the things you might need for the next few hours. Next, you had to be sure the car seat was buckled in securely before you loaded your precious cargo. Then, you were off and running. You didn't encounter anyone who had even the slightest cold, and you actually made it back home all in one piece. Why not enjoy a little salute to the success of the first outing—and to making it back home? The Holland House Martini is a nice gin cocktail, with a dash of maraschino liqueur and splash of vermouth, which feels an awful lot like home. Make it ice cold and relax.

The Reward: *Holland House Martini*
Makes 1 martini

> 1¾ ounces Jenever (use dry gin if that's all you have on hand)
> ¾ ounce dry vermouth
> ¼ ounce maraschino liqueur
> ½ ounce lemon juice
> Garnish: lemon twist

Combine all liquid ingredients in an ice-filled cocktail shaker. Shake vigorously for about 20 seconds. Strain into a chilled martini glass and garnish.

Thank You for Being a Friend Martini

The Feat: *Made a New Friend at Mommy and Me*

Moms can often get isolated, spending every waking moment with their kids. So when you had a chance to make a new friend, you jumped on it. You started going to those Mommy and Me sessions for some support and—hopefully—advice, when needed. The fact that you met another mom whom you clicked with is the icing on the cake. Now you have a friend to call when you're at your wits' end and need someone to talk you off the ledge . . . and it goes without saying that you'll do the same for her. From taking walks with the kids, to coordinating playdates, to offering to babysit for each other, this friendship has potential to go the long haul. So cheers to having a new friend! Cheers to being able to have actual adult conversation! And cheers to the martini called Golden Friendship! In honor of your newfound buddy, mix up a martini to cement the deal. It's slightly sweet and bubbly, which means it's perfect for an afternoon toast. Make two and invite your friend over to try it.

The Reward: *Golden Friendship*
Makes 1 martini

1 ounce light rum
1 ounce sweet vermouth
1 ounce amaretto
3 ounces ginger ale
Garnish: 1 cherry

Pour rum, vermouth, and amaretto into a shaker half filled with ice. Shake and strain into a martini glass. Add ginger ale to fill and garnish with a cherry.

You're on My List Martini

The Feat: *Left the House Without Forgetting Something*

Feeling like a pack mule is just going to be a part of your life for the near future. With kids going from point A to point B, you're the one who has to remember to bring everything. It starts with the diaper bag and goes on to include dance clothes, sports gear, homework, and bake sale goodies. From the first trip home from the hospital, through high school graduation, you are the keeper and carrier of all things. Yet it seems like no matter how hard you try, there's always one item left behind. But today you achieved the simple, satisfying goal of remembering everything. Yes, everything! You almost want to do a little dance to celebrate the moment. Go ahead, no one is watching! Now, to make sure you don't spoil your luck, make up the Knock on Wood martini. In this cocktail, the Scotch and peach flavors come together to make a smoky, sweet taste you won't soon forget.

The Reward: *Knock on Wood*
Makes 1 martini

2 ounces Scotch
½ ounce peach schnapps
½ ounce Madeira
3 dashes peach bitters

Pour all ingredients into a shaker half filled with ice. Shake and strain into a chilled martini glass.

Cruise-Control Cocktail

The Feat: *Chauffeured Baby from Point A to Point B, Without Driving off the Road*

New parents really ought to receive a special commemoration from the DMV. Because driving with a baby in the car—wrangling the kid into an infant seat, using your rearview mirror as a baby monitor, and, oh yeah, not fender-bending along the way—is some A-for-effort, extra-credit, get-a-gold-star kind of driving. It's almost James Bond–level driving, come to think of it, which is why the Vesper—which was invented by 007 himself in *Casino Royale*—is the perfect martini for some postroad nerve-soothing: True to Bond's preference for "shaken, not stirred," this recipe's instructions are tailored accordingly.

The Reward: *Vesper*

Makes 1 martini

> 3 ounces gin
> 1 ounce vodka
> ½ ounce Lillet Blanc
> Garnish: lemon peel

Pour your gin, vodka, and Lillet into an ice-filled cocktail shaker. Shake vigorously for about 20 seconds. Strain into a chilled martini glass and add garnish.

Come Fly with Me Martini

The Feat: *Successfully Traveled with Your Baby on a Plane*

With more and more relatives scattered cross-country these days, more and more newborns are taking to the skies. Unfortunately, this can mean more and more headaches for you. It's hard enough to pack everything your little one needs for a day out of the house, but a trip across the country is nearly impossible. But you were prepared. You brought plenty of treats and toys to occupy your baby in every effort to eliminate onboard meltdowns. You even brought a few goodies for those sitting around you as a pre-emptive "thank you for understanding babies sometimes cry" gesture. You definitely earned your wings on this trip. How should you celebrate? Enter The Aviator martini. Like many classic cocktails of murky origins, there's more than one accepted recipe for making an Aviator. A perfect martini (gin with equal parts sweet and dry vermouth), with a dash of Dubonnet (a French aperitif), is one way. The recipe below is another—and it's a much more daring—and thus, much more fitting—drink to commemorate your up-in-the-air adventure.

The Reward: *The Aviator*
Makes 1 martini

2 ounces dry gin	Egg white from a medium-sized
½ ounce maraschino liqueur	egg
½ ounce lemon juice	¼ ounce Crème de cassis

Pour gin, maraschino liqueur, lemon juice, and egg white into a cocktail shaker without ice and shake vigorously for about 20 seconds. Then add ice and shake for another 20 seconds. Strain into a chilled martini glass. Finish off the drink by pouring your Crème de cassis into the center of the drink; it will sink to the bottom of the glass's V-shaped bowl, giving the drink a layered look.

The Road Trip-tini

The Feat: *Returned Home from a Family Road Trip with Your Sanity Intact*

Road trips are cost-effective ways to travel, and they can make family vacations a reality instead of just a dream. But actually taking one of those road trips can sometimes turn into a nightmare. Think about it: You were all crammed into the car for countless hours watching the mile markers go by along the highway. Everyone wanted to eat something different, use the bathroom at a different time, and stop at different sites along the way. And if you had to hear, "Are we there yet?" one more time, your head might have exploded. Yet you survived the trip with no major car repairs, no visits to the emergency room, and your sanity still intact. All in all, that's considered road trip success. You also have a lot of great memories and a few decent photos you can share with friends and family. But before you start planning for the next trip, take a moment to mark the success of this one with the Flat Tire at the Border martini. Enjoy this one whether you had a flat tire or not. After all, everything is flexible when it comes to road trips.

The Reward: *Flat Tire at the Border*
Makes 1 martini

> 2 ounces blanco tequila
> 1 ounce black sambuca

Pour all ingredients into a shaker half filled with ice. Shake and strain into a chilled martini glass.

A Camping Cocktail

The Feat: *Survived the First Family Camping Trip*

A family camping trip can be a lot of fun. You packed up the kids, tents, and sleeping bags and headed off into the wild for the weekend. Okay, maybe it was only a professional campsite with real showers and hot water, but it's still camping if you slept in a tent. So, when you sat around the campfire making s'mores (another requirement), you basked in the warm memories you were creating. Hopefully those warm memories fought off the cold that seeped into your sleeping bag in the middle of the night. And, maybe they numbed you to the pain you felt lying on the ground on top of what you're sure was a pile of rocks. You got up early, cooked over that open fire, and washed dishes in a bucket, all with a smile because family camping trips are fun (you kept repeating to yourself over and over). Finally, as you pulled out of the campsite and headed home, stiff, sore, and smelling of smoke, you realized that you survived! Now it's time for your reward, a S'moretini! Complete with a graham cracker rim, it's just the drink to celebrate your pioneer spirit.

The Reward: *S'moretini*

Makes 1 martini

1½ ounces marshmallow vodka	Garnish: chocolate syrup
¾ ounce dark crème de cacao	Garnish: crushed graham crackers
½ ounce Licor 43	Garnish: skewered mini
½ ounce light cream	marshmallows

Pour your vodka, crème de cacao, Licor 43, and cream into an ice-filled shaker. Shake vigorously for about 20 seconds. Swirl chocolate syrup into and on the rim of a chilled martini glass. Dip the rim of the glass into the crushed graham crackers. Pour the contents of the shaker into the glass and garnish with a skewer of mini marshmallows.

S'moretini

It's Only Make Believe-tini

The Feat: *Made the Pilgrimage to Disney*

If you have kids, at some point you're going to be asked, or begged, to go to Disney. After all, who doesn't love the Happiest Place on Earth? That's why you planned and saved until you could take your kids. Watching those little faces look up in wonder at everything and everyone around them was priceless, and creating a memory that will last a lifetime was worth the long lines for all the rides, overpriced food, and souvenirs. You know that the Land of Make Believe is all gears, motors, and actors, but who cares? To your children it was all fairytales, characters, and magic—just the way it should be. Here's a toast to fantasies, and to you, for making this one come true for your kids. Enjoy a bubbly martini called the Make Believe. Gingery sweet and super bubbly, this toddy will tickle your fancy and make you believe in magic one more time.

 The Reward: *Make Believe*

Makes 1 martini

¼ **ounce dark rum**
¼ **ounce ginger syrup**
¼ **ounce fresh lime juice**
2½ **ounces dry champagne**

Pour all ingredients into a martini glass and gently stir.

Home for the Holidays Martini

The Feat: *Traveled as a Family for the Holidays and Lived to Tell the Tale*

Traveling is hard enough, but traveling as a family is extra stressful. Add the holidays to the mix and you may not live to tell the tale. But this year, not only did you survive, you made the most of it and had a good time. You handled all the reservations and negotiations for your brood while keeping everyone (mostly) happy. And when someone wasn't happy, you managed to avoid any out-and-out breakdowns, meltdowns, and fist fights. The world is going to want your secrets. And best of all, you all made it home in one piece and are still on speaking terms with the rest of your family. Compared to some of the war stories you've heard, your trip was as easy as apple pie . . . and, doesn't a nice warm, homey, apple pie sound good right about now? Fortunately, you don't have to bake anything, just whip up the scrumptious Apple Pie martini, and pat yourself on the back for realizing that there's no place like home for the holidays!

 The Reward: *Apple Pie*

Makes 1 martini

2 ounces rum
1 ounce sweet vermouth
½ ounce apple brandy
2 ounces lemon juice or juice of ½ lemon
Splash grenadine

Pour all ingredients into a shaker with ice. Shake well and strain into a martini glass.

Life's a Beach . . . and It's Full of Sand Cocktail

The Feat: *Survived a Beach Trip/Day at the Beach*

Anyone who refers to something easy as "a day at the beach" has never spent a day at the beach with a child. First of all, you had to pack everything you might ever need, plus something to sit on, and then cram it all into the car. Then you loaded the car with all the passengers, which in and of itself is not an easy task. After a drive that took twice as long as you planned, because everyone else wanted to go to the beach too, you arrived and found a parking spot. Because you don't have a pack mule, you lugged all your items to the beach and claimed a little spot of sand. Of course, that sand then got into everything from sunscreen to sandwiches, but still, you kept everyone covered in lotion and watched the kids play along the water's edge. You even managed to relax for a moment or two, before it was time to load it all up and head back home. Everyone had a great time, but you're exhausted. Well, in a salute to you, whip up the Waikiki Beachcomber-tini and think, "Surf's up!"

The Reward: *Waikiki Beachcomber-tini*

Makes 2 martinis

1½ ounces vodka
4 ounces guava juice
1 ounce lime juice or juice of ½ lime
½ ounce raspberry liqueur

Pour vodka, guava juice, and lime juice into a shaker half filled with ice. Shake well and strain into martini glasses. Float the liqueur on top.

Waikiki Beachcomber-tini

One Hot Mama Martini

The Feat: *Floated Through a Trip to the Neighborhood Pool in Midsummer*

It's a fact that most women gain weight when they have kids. So when you got the invitation to the neighborhood pool party, you started to panic. What would you wear? Did you even have a decent bathing suit to try on? How much weight could a person lose in three weeks? Then you remembered that there would be other moms at the party dealing with the same thing. You also reconnected with the reality that you are *so much more* than the size of your swimsuit. So when the time came, you donned your tropical best, slapped on your flip flops, and strutted to the poolside. You had so much fun that you were a bit disappointed when the party ended. Keep the festivities going back home by shaking up a tropical concoction that fits how you feel. The luscious Bahama Mama Martini is fruity and fabulous, just like you!

The Reward: *Bahama Mama Martini*

Makes 1 martini

½ ounce light rum
½ ounce dark rum
1 ounce piña colada mix
1 ounce bar punch mix (a mix of orange juice, pineapple juice, sour mix, and grenadine)
Garnish: 1 pineapple slice
Garnish: 1 cherry

Pour all ingredients, except garnishes, into a shaker half filled with ice. Shake vigorously, and then pour into a martini glass. Garnish with pineapple slice and cherry.

Bahama Mama Martini

The Red in the Face Cocktail

The Feat: *Wore the Title of "Most Embarrassing Mom" with Pride*

It's a little bit like the chicken and egg theory. You're not sure which came first: your child not wanting to be seen with you, or you embarrassed her in public. Either way, your work here is done. No matter how much you want to deny it, there comes a time when your kid is completely humiliated by the very fact that you're her mom. It's something that countless moms before you have tried to avoid, all to no avail. You know it's just a phase, but you still have to serve your time in "uncool parent" purgatory, which is why you figured that, if you had to wear the title, you wanted to earn it. Today, you gave it your best and truly succeeded in making your girl turn beet red! Later—many years later—you'll both laugh about where you showed up and what you were wearing, but for now, your title stands as World's Most Embarrassing Mom. Standing there like the "old square" your child thinks you are, raise a glass of Vieux Carre, and be proud. Why the Vieux Carre? Easy! This French term for what we call New Orleans's French Quarter translates to "old square," which means you're in good company! Enjoy!

 The Reward: *Vieux Carre*

Makes 1 martini

1½ ounces rye whiskey
1½ ounces brandy
1½ ounces sweet vermouth
¼ ounce Benedictine
2 dashes Peychaud Bitters
2 dashes bitters

Pour all ingredients into a shaker half filled with ice. Shake and strain into martini glasses.

Vieux Carre

The Two Tickets to Paradise-tini

The Feat: *Went on an Adult-Only, Weekend Getaway*

It's hard to believe it actually happened but you were able to break away for an adult-only weekend! You didn't think too much about how everything magically fell into place, because that might have broken the spell and ruined the trip. Instead, you just enjoyed some time away from carpools and graham crackers, and recharged your batteries. Every parent, especially a mom, needs a break every once in a while. Usually you're grateful for an afternoon here or there, so the weekend getaway was like Christmas and Easter all rolled into one. You ate at restaurants that weren't kid-friendly, went dancing, and just did whatever struck your fancy. Regardless of how you spent your time, you are still giddy about the fact that you actually got an entire weekend away from the responsibilities that come along with being a mom. Yes, you missed your children and were glad to hug them when you got home, but you're already thinking about planning another trip. That's where the Charming Proposal martini comes into play. So shake up the schnapps and pour in the passion, because this martini is almost as charming as your weekend getaway.

The Reward: *Charming Proposal*
Makes 1 martini

1 ounce sour apple schnapps
¼ ounce grenadine
1 ounce passionfruit liqueur
Ginger ale, to fill

Pour the first three ingredients into a shaker half filled with ice. Shake and strain into a chilled martini glass. Fill with the ginger ale.

Chapter 10
Festive Feats

From birthday parties to holiday gatherings, there's nothing like a festive day to send a mom over the edge. All that planning and cleaning and cooking and cleaning and decorating and cleaning . . . whew, no wonder you're exhausted! But as a mom, you are always working hard to make each family celebration the absolute best it can be, and that deserves some recognition. Whether it's the family photo for the Christmas card or making Halloween costumes with garbage bags and duct tape, you make it happen. When your kids grow up and move away, you will be at the center of every holiday memory. And when they have their own festivities, they're going to want to do it "just like Mom did." In honor of that awesome job you always do, enjoy one or two (or more!) of the festive martini recipes found in this chapter. No need to wrap them up or make them fancy, just make one quick, because another holiday is right around the corner.

Have Your Cake and Drink It, Too

The Feat: *Made It Through Your Kid's First Birthday Party*

Throwing your child's first birthday party is a big deal. These days there's a lot of pressure to have spectacular events of epic proportions, and the bar keeps getting raised higher and higher. From the theme to the entertainment to the party favors, every detail matters. It's enough to exhaust you before the party day even arrives. But, you did it! You planned, invited, and hosted an amazing, festive party . . . even the other parents were impressed. Of course, the first birthday party you throw for your child needn't be for your child's first birthday. In fact, considering the fact that a twelve-month-old guest of honor does not know what a present is, cannot make it through an afternoon without a nap, and enjoys destroying cake as much as eating it, this milestone may be one you wisely hold off on for an extra year or two. Regardless of when you throw this gala event, there's a lot of work involved. So, even if you're just in the planning stages, you deserve a reward for stepping up to the plate. Why not throw some birthday cake on that plate, grown-up style, with the Birthday Cake Martini?

The Reward: *Birthday Cake Martini*
Makes 1 martini

Powdered sugar (for rim)	Splash lemon juice
2 ounces cherry brandy	Garnish: sprinkles
1½ ounces dark crème de cacao	Garnish: maraschino cherries
½ ounce Benedictine	

Sugar the rim of your martini glass and set aside. Pour your brandy, crème de cacao, Benedictine, and juice into an ice-filled cocktail shaker, and shake vigorously for about 20 seconds. Strain into your martini glass. Before adding your cherries to garnish, coat them with sprinkles by shaking sprinkles and cherries together in a sandwich bag, or roll cherries atop a sprinkle-covered saucer.

Birthday Cake Martini

Happy Birthday to Me Martini

The Feat: *Threw a Birthday Party for Yourself*

Some moms have decided to age gracefully and some go into each birthday kicking and screaming. Regardless of which one describes you, celebrating the day you were born is a must! So this year, it was time to throw a party for you. No, not the kind of party with clowns and party favors, a real grown-up party for a real grown up—you! Maybe you went to your favorite restaurant or maybe you farmed the kids out to a babysitter and had cocktails at the house. The type of party you hosted isn't important, but the fact that you took a moment to celebrate you sure is! It really is okay to focus on yourself for a few hours every once in a while, and your birthday is the perfect time to do just that. So raise a glass filled with an Aged Manhattan; like you, the whiskey in this martini just gets better with age.

The Reward: *Aged Manhattan*
Makes 1 martini

2 ounces aged bourbon whiskey
1 ounce sweet vermouth
2 dashes bitters
Garnish: 1 cherry

Pour all ingredients, except garnish, into a shaker with ice. Shake and strain into a martini glass to serve. Garnish with a cherry.

Living in a Fantasy Martini

The Feat: *Helped Your Child Believe In the Easter Bunny/Santa Claus/Tooth Fairy for Another Year*

Just one more year is all you want, right? What can be the harm in allowing your kid to have another twelve months to believe in magical things? Whether it was Santa Claus, the Easter Bunny, the tooth fairy, or all of the above, you decided that this fantasy will stay in place for now. Good for you, Mom, your child is growing up fast enough. But even more impressive was how you danced around all the questions and gave the right answers to put to rest the things other kids might be telling your child. Sure, maybe it's all smoke and mirrors, but you are a true expert with both. You can take pride in your fancy footwork as you go about setting things up for that next holiday or special occasion. In honor of your powers, why not enjoy the Smoke and Mirrors martini while you're at it. A unique blend of Scotch, absinthe, and simple syrup, the flavor is as magical as the myth of Santa Claus, the Easter Bunny, and the tooth fairy. Cheers to them all.

The Reward: *Smoke and Mirrors*
Makes 1 martini

> 2 ounces Scotch
> 1 ounce absinthe
> ½ ounce simple syrup
> ½ ounce fresh lime juice

Pour all ingredients into a shaker half filled with ice. Shake and strain into a martini glass.

Now Where Did I Put That Martini

The Feat: *Remembered Where You Hid That Last, Lost Easter Egg*

Every Easter, after the wonderful Easter egg hunt, someone would count the eggs and realize there was one lone, lost egg still out there somewhere. You looked everywhere that you remembered hiding them and quizzed the kids to be sure no one was pulling a fast one. Still, no missing egg was found. Well, maybe you just counted wrong and life had to go on. However, months later it came to you. So you unwrapped this foil-covered chocolate egg to see how it faired tucked away in the closet for so many months. The answer is not too well. You know how chocolate gets sort of white when it gets old? That's what happened here. Obviously you have to toss it out, but now you're craving chocolate. Forget the eggs and whip up this white chocolate wonder, in honor of the now-white chocolate egg.

The Reward: *White Chocolate Easter-tini*

Makes 1 martini

1 ounce vanilla vodka
1 ounce white chocolate liqueur
2 ounces eggnog
1 ounce cream
Garnish: jellybeans

Pour all liquids into a martini shaker of ice. Shake, then strain into a martini glass. Hide your little Easter eggs by dropping some jellybeans in the glass to sink to the bottom.

Tie Another One On Martini

The Feat: *Helped Your Kid Pick Out Another Father's Day Necktie for Dad*

You know he has more neckties than he can shake a stick at, but taking your child out shopping for Father's Day and selecting a silky selection of stripes or paisley—or whatever the latest trend might be—is practically a tradition at this point. You chuckle to yourself because you know how the man feels about ties, but you also know he'd be slightly disappointed if he didn't get his annual gift. And while you're not the one who is going to wear it, you *are* the one who spends what feels like hours picking it out. Your child is particular to say the least, agonizing over which one is truly the best choice. Finally, with the selection made and the immediately recognizable box all wrapped up with ribbon and a bow, you can check another item off the to-do list. Now you can relax and have a bit of time for yourself. The perfect concoction for today is the Aggravation martini. Raise your Scotch and coffee-liqueur cocktail to the aggravation of shopping for your partner's tie.

 The Reward: *Aggravation*
Makes 1 martini

2 ounces blended Scotch whiskey
1 ounce coffee liqueur

Pour all ingredients into a shaker of ice. Shake thoroughly and strain into a martini glass.

Light Up the Night Martini

The Feat: *Went Out to See Fireworks*

Summer is a great time of year . . . longer days, warmer weather, and fireworks! But enjoying those explosions of color and light isn't as easy as it used to be as most neighborhoods won't let you light up the bottle rockets in the backyard. It makes sense, and you're all for safety first, but seeing that annual patriotic fireworks display is something you want your kids to experience, just like you did. Okay, maybe it can't be just like you did, but you can drive them to the local park or waterfront to enjoy the show. Easy as apple pie, right? Umm . . . not so much. First you had to pack the car with blankets and snacks and kids—a feat in and of itself. Then it was fighting traffic to get there, finding a parking spot that wasn't a mile away, and finally, toting everything to the ideal vantage point. But, wow, you did it! You arrived early, enjoyed a picnic and settled in for the show. Amid the fiery lights exploding in the sky, you got to hear the "oohs" and "aahs" from your kids, and the night was as magical as you remembered. Now, with everyone safely home, it's time to seal your day and celebrate your accomplishment with a patriotic martini.

The Reward: *Born on the Fourth of July Martini*
Makes 1 martini

1½ ounces cherry vodka or rum
3 ounces white (clear) cranberry juice
Garnish: 1 maraschino cherry
½ ounce blue curaçao

Pour the cherry vodka or rum and the white (clear) cranberry juice into a martini shaker of ice. Shake and strain into a martini glass. Drop the cherry in to sink to the bottom; then carefully float the blue curaçao on top by pouring it over the back of a spoon.

Move Over Martha-tini

The Feat: *Sewed (or Scotch Taped) a Homemade Halloween Costume*

Maybe sewing was never your strong suit, but you were determined to put together a homemade Halloween costume for your kid. After all, it only had to last one night. Out came the fleece, old sheets, ribbons, and buttons, and you became a costume-making machine. You actually enjoyed yourself as your creation came to life. Who knew if it would fit? You just hoped it looked something like the image that you and your child envisioned at the start of the project . . . and you know what, it turned out okay. Maybe you had to pin, tape, and staple in a few places, but the costume was finished and your kid was ready to go trick-or-treating in style. When the designated parent came to collect your festooned wonder to wander the streets with the neighborhood kids, you stood proud and smiled. After you put away the project supplies, you deserve a moment of recognition for another mom-task completed. In honor of Halloween, enjoy the Wicked Witch martini. The coffee liqueur, crème, and vodka treat doesn't require a shaker, but a steady hand and a spoon. For someone who can create a costume like you, it's no trick at all.

 The Reward: *Wicked Witch*

Makes 1 martini

1 ounce coffee liqueur
1 ounce white crème de cacao
1 ounce black vodka

Into a martini glass, layer each ingredient, in order, by pouring over a spoon.

No More Candy for You Martini

The Feat: *Didn't Eat Your Kid's Halloween Candy*

Is there anything more tempting than candy—especially that gooey, yummy kind that your kid brings home on Halloween? You've managed to get the amount of candy you buy down to a science so that there's none left in the house once the trick-or-treaters have gone home, but your kid's candy is another thing entirely. First of all, there's so much. How many houses did he make it to anyway? The next problem is that if you leave the candy in his bedroom, there won't be anything left in the morning except a very sick boy. So, is it better to hide it or have it out in the open? Well, you promised you wouldn't eat any this year and you're going to stick to your guns. Good for you! You managed to oversee the doling out of sweets to your sweet, while resisting overwhelming temptation to pop a treat or two in your mouth. Now, it's time to celebrate your willpower with a grown-up treat—the Peanut Butter Cup martini.

The Reward: *Peanut Butter Cup*

Makes 1 martini

1½ ounces vodka
1½ ounces CocoRibe
1 scoop vanilla ice cream
2 tablespoons peanut butter (chunky)
2 tablespoons chocolate syrup

Pour ingredients in a blender. Blend until smooth and pour into a martini glass. Drink with a straw.

Peanut Butter Cup

Holiday House Party Martini

The Feat: *Hosted a Holiday Soiree at Home*

You love the idea of having a holiday party in your own home, but you just hate the stress of trying to get everything perfect. This year you figured it out; you don't have to be perfect! You just had to be yourself, be happy, and enjoy the holidays with friends. That meant whatever decorations were up by party time were good enough, and as for the rest of the house, well, no one is supposed to be peeking into the bedrooms anyway. You just dimmed the lights, lit the candles, and turned on the holiday tunes. Your personal spread of snacks, or the last-minute potluck buffet, was perfect because people love food—period. And whether you share it with the crowd or savor it after the guests have all gone home, you deserve the perfect holiday drink to revel in your soiree success. Enter the classy and classic Eggnog Grog martini!

The Reward: *Eggnog Grog*
Makes 1 martini

> 1½ ounces dark rum
> Cold eggnog, to fill
> Garnish: nutmeg

Pour the dark rum into a chilled martini glass and fill with eggnog. Garnish with a pinch of nutmeg on top.

Eggnog Grog

The Longest Line Martini

The Feat: *Took Your Kid to the Mall to Meet Santa*

Taking your kid to meet Santa is a holiday tradition you want to continue as long as you can. Children grow up and Christmas changes, but for now, you have your mop-top anxiously waiting to see the fat man in the red suit. Dressed in holiday finery, you bundled everyone into the car for a trip to what can best be described as holiday hell . . . the mall. It's not that malls are so bad; it's just that they get so crowded with crazy folks during this time of year. People are supposed to be happier, but crowded stores and long lines can make even the cheeriest elf a little snarky. So you pack your patience and head to the longest line of all . . . the line to meet Santa Claus. Your kid wants to tell Santa what to bring and you want just one decent photo for your family. After what seems like hours, your child hops up on Santa's lap and you get your holiday pic! Finally back home and away from the crowds, reward yourself for keeping the Christmas spirit and sip on this chocolate-peppermint holiday martini. Here's to a White Christmas!

 ## The Reward: *White Christmas*
Makes 1 martini

> 1½ ounces vanilla-flavored vodka
> 1 ounce Godiva White Chocolate Liqueur
> 1 ounce peppermint schnapps

Pour all ingredients into a shaker with ice. Stir and strain into a chilled martini glass.

The Family Vogue-tini

The Feat: *Took an Acceptable Holiday Card Photo*

You've always marveled at those Norman Rockwell–ish family photos that others send in their holiday greetings. How in the world do they get everyone in matching outfits looking so perfect and pristine? With your shots, you're just happy when everyone's eyes are open. Well this year, you vowed, would be different. Weeks of planning outfits and poses and location went into it. Finally the day arrived with the usual fiascos, but you persevered and didn't give up. Eventually, all that work paid off and everyone was wearing the right clothes, in the right place, at the right time so you started to take some pictures before things started to fall apart. Later on, you scrolled through your takes, getting more and more discouraged. But wait, what was that one? All eyes open, everyone looking at the camera, with smiles. Could it be? Yes it is . . . your holiday photo! You took a deep breath and felt grateful, and now you were going to celebrate. It's time for a kiss . . . a Cranberry Kiss!

The Reward: *Cranberry Kiss*
Makes 1 martini

¾ ounce spiced rum
½ ounce peppermint schnapps
2 ounces Collins mix
2 ounces cranberry juice
Garnish: lime slice

Pour all ingredients, except garnish, into a shaker of ice. Shake and strain into a chilled martini glass. Garnish with a lime slice.

Missing Parts Martini

The Feat: *Assembled the Some-Assembly-Required Toy*

Every year you say the same thing: no more assembling toys on Christmas Eve. Yet, there you were again, trying to be sure you had all the parts and looking for the instructions written in a language you could actually read. It was late and you were tired, but there was no rest until the night-before to-do list was complete. Knee deep in bolts, screws, and toggles—and a few things you didn't know what to call—you assembled part A and attached it to part B. There were a few moments of utter exasperation, and you almost threw in the towel twice, but you stuck with it and now you see the fruits of your labor. Not too shabby, if you do say so yourself. In the morning you'll have a very happy child, which just might make up for the backache you'll also have when you wake up. Until then, it's time to finish up that to-do list which includes indulging yourself in a much-deserved holiday treat. It might not make sugar plums dance in your head, but the Nutcracker Sweet martini will help you get through the rest of the night.

The Reward: *Nutcracker Sweet*
Makes 2 martinis

2 ounces vodka
2 ounces Kahlúa
2 ounces Irish cream liqueur
2 ounces amaretto

Pour all ingredients into a shaker with ice. Shake and strain into martini glasses.

The Downhill Racer Martini

The Feat: *Went Sledding with Your Kid*

You know you're not as flexible as you used to be and you know your back is going to hurt later, but, Mom, you did it anyway. You went sledding with your kid . . . and that makes you a snowy superhero. You know it wouldn't have been any fun for her to sled on her own and there was no way she could drag that sled back up the hill for each run. So, you buttoned up, booted up, and braved that hill for some sloppy, sloshy, icy thrills. The cool thing is that once you got started, you had more fun than you thought you would. And seeing your daughter's face, flushed red with cold, but still grinning from ear to ear . . . that's the good stuff! So you stuck it out until you were both frozen stiff and had to pack it in for the day. Now, your little girl is in the other room thawing out with a mug of hot cocoa, but what about you? Martinis! While the hot chocolate mix is still out, whip up a tasty treat that just might put you in the mood to sled again tomorrow. Okay, probably not, but it's still delicious! Enjoy.

 ## The Reward: *Hot Cocoa*
Makes 2 martinis

1½ tablespoons hot chocolate mix
1½ ounces dark rum
1½ ounces dark crème de cacao
4½ ounces cream or milk

Dip the rims of the martini glasses in water, and then dip them into the powdered hot chocolate mix. Pour the rum, crème de cacao, and cream or milk into a martini shaker of ice. Shake and strain into rimmed martini glasses.

Hot Cocoa

The Snowman Martini

The Feat: *Built a Snowman with Your Kids*

There's something about the first snow of the season that brings out the kid in all of us. And on this snowy weekend (or school snow day) you were almost giddy with excitement. You decided to forget about watching weather updates all day, and figured the movies could wait until dark. Now was the time for you to bond with your kids over the current task at hand . . . building a snowman! You totally got into it as you rummaged around for hats, scarves, and gloves, and you and your kids rushed outside to roll snowballs that would become your masterpiece. And, being the amazing mom you are, you let the kids take the lead in designing your icy creation. Once the most amazing snowman ever was complete, and you took pictures to commemorate your handiwork, you realized you were frozen to the bone. Frostbite hadn't actually set in, but it sure felt like it could happen at any moment. Inside, it was warm blankets and beverages for everyone . . . everyone but you that is. Why? Because your exploits require something a bit more apropos to take off the chill: a delicious martini called The Frostbite.

The Reward: *The Frostbite*

Makes 1 martini

2 ounces tequila
1½ ounces white crème de cacao
1½ ounces cream
Garnish: dash of nutmeg

Pour all ingredients, except garnish, into a shaker with ice. Shake hard and strain into a martini glass. Garnish with a dash of nutmeg.

The Arts and Crafts Cocktail

The Feat: *Organized Family Photo Album and Scrapbook*

You have soared beyond other moms and reached the impossible dream. That's right; you organized your family photo album and scrapbook. Most moms have boxes and envelopes of photos and memorabilia that do nothing more than collect dust. But night after night, you pulled out the boxes and chipped away at organizing memories. Your kids may not yet understand the value of what you've done, but in the years to come, they will say thank you. Until then, you still get to brag to all your friends and family who have yet to reach your level of scrapbook diva-ness. As you sit back and behold the glory that is your family photo album, realize you've achieved a dream. That's why the perfect cocktail for the occasion is The Golden Dream, an orangy, creamy martini that goes down easier than those photos and ticket stubs on the scrapbook page. No glue required, just shake, pour, and enjoy.

 The Reward: *The Golden Dream*
Makes 1 martini

1 ounce cream
1 ounce orange juice
1 ounce Cointreau
1 ounce Galliano

Pour all ingredients into a shaker with ice. Shake well and strain into a chilled martini glass.

Chapter 11
Kids Will Be Kids Feats

Kids are busy, and that means moms are busy too. Not only do you have your list of to-dos and chores to get done every day, you also take time to play with your kids, entertain your kids, and sneak in as much quality time as possible. From making macaroni art with your daughter to letting your son build a blanket fort in the living room, you understand that play is very serious business. You also get that some of life's biggest lessons are learned through games and activities, which is why you work so hard to let your children have fun.

For all the macaroni art, Girl Scout meetings, and movie watching (their pick, not yours), this chapter says, "Thanks for playing." And as a bit of a parting gift, here you'll find delicious cocktails to celebrate the way you nurture your child's imagination and sense of play. The martini recipes we've included here use vodkas, rums, and even yogurt (but not all in one drink), so let your taste buds guide you. Experiment a little and have some fun for yourself as you rest up between playdates.

The Dog Gone Martini

The Feat: *Finally Broke Down and Got a Puppy*

For many households, there comes a time when a puppy enters the mix. The process usually starts when a kid, like yours, asks time and again for a four-legged, furry sibling. You, of course, listed all the reasons that it didn't make sense to get a puppy, but your child assured you that he would take care of the puppy every day. You went down the list of duties: feeding, walking, brushing, washing, and training, and he eagerly agreed to every single one. He looked up at you with those puppy dog eyes of his own and you finally broke down. You said "yes" to the puppy and made your son's dreams of loyal companionship come true. What's so great is that you said "yes" knowing you would end up handling the bulk of the dog-care responsibilities. Especially, you were sure, the slobbery, stinky jobs. But even with all that, you knew how much your boy would love a dog and you had to say "yes." But before the household dynamic changes for good, you need to enjoy some quiet time. The martini best suited for the job? The Greyhound Martini, of course!

The Reward: *The Greyhound Martini*

Makes 1 martini

1½ ounces vodka
Grapefruit juice

Pour vodka into a shaker half filled with ice. Shake and strain into a chilled martini glass. Add grapefruit juice to fill.

The Greyhound Martini

The Perfect Playdate Martini

The Feat: *Hosted a Playdate*

It was your turn to host the playdate for your tot and her best friend. But you decided to more than simply host, and helped them have a magical tea party. First you provided dress up clothes. Then you set them up with all the trimmings for a perfect tea party table, complete with milk for tea, graham crackers for cookies, and yogurt for their sweet but good-for-you dessert. Once they were dressed up and ready to go, you left them to it. You could tell by all the giggles and chatting that everything was going well and you could relax with a successful playdate well under your belt. Nice work, Mom. When the playdate was done, it was your time. What's on the list? Get some chores done? Cuddle up on the sofa to read a book? Better yet, how about using the yogurt and graham crackers to make an amazing cocktail: the Key Lime Pie martini.

The Reward: *Key Lime Pie*
Makes 1 martini

Juice from ½ lime
Kosher salt
Crushed graham crackers
1½ ounces tequila
½ ounce key lime crème liqueur
3 ounces key lime yogurt
Garnish: lime wedge

Rub the lime juice around the rim of a martini glass and set extra aside. Dip half the rim in kosher salt, half in the graham crackers. Pour the tequila, key lime crème liqueur, key lime yogurt, and remainder of lime juice into a shaker of ice. Shake vigorously until well-blended. Pour into martini glass and garnish with the lime wedge.

Key Lime Pie

Tickle the Ivories Martini

The Feat: *Taught Your Kid to Play "Chopsticks"*

It may not be anyone's first sing-along song, but that's only because there are no lyrics. Still, "Chopsticks" has to be the first song that everyone's played on the piano—and, you just taught your child that classic two-fingered tune. What fun it was as you watched his face light up when he made actual music come from the piano. Over and over, you showed him the keys until finally he memorized and played it solo. You both laughed in delight as "Chopsticks" echoed through the house. He is still playing it over and over again, and you're beginning to wonder if you'll rue this day, but that's a thought for tomorrow. Right now, you're basking in your boy's brilliance at the keyboard and wondering if you should sign him up for lessons. Maybe you should start saving money for Juilliard? You decide to wait to see if he learns any other songs before you make that call, and, for now, you just sit back and bask in the warmth of how well you taught him and how easily he learned. You are a maestro and deserve a beverage to match your mood. So get out the rum and cream sherry and shake yourself a Maestro martini!

The Reward: *Maestro*

Makes 2 martinis

1½ ounces Añejo rum
½ ounce cream sherry
½ ounce lime juice
4 ounces ginger ale
Garnish: lemon twist

Pour the rum, sherry, and lime juice into a shaker half filled with ice. Shake well and strain into a chilled martini glass. Top off with the ginger ale. Garnish with a lemon twist.

The Fort-ifier Martini

The Feat: *Let Your Kids Destroy the Living Room to Make a Blanket Fort*

It was raining outside and the kids were bored. Rather than have them spend the afternoon in front of the television or playing on the computer, you were thrilled to let them make a fort in the living room. You moved anything fragile or breakable, so there was nothing to worry about and they could just let loose. You even pulled out blankets, sheets, and pillows for them to use, because that's the kind of mom you are. Then you left them alone with their imaginations. The laughter you heard was a sure sign that you had done the right thing. You did sneak back in with some snacks that were eagerly accepted, but you quickly left, as you had to honor the "No Mom Zone." Fair enough. Simply scoot out to the other room and have a mom's only treat . . . the Beach Blanket Bingo martini. In honor of having fun and to celebrate the blanket fort, just raise a glass!

The Reward: *Beach Blanket Bingo*
Makes 1 martini

1 ounce light rum
2 ounces white grape juice
1½ ounces cranberry juice
Club soda
Garnish: 1 lemon slice
Garnish: 1 lime slice
Garnish: 1 cherry

Pour rum and juices into a shaker half filled with ice. Shake and strain into a chilled martini glass. Add club soda to fill. Garnish with a slice of lemon, a slice of lime, and a cherry.

Get a Charge Out of It Martini

The Feat: *Changed Batteries in a Toy*

Your child comes to you with a battery-operated toy that's not working . . . and you know what you have to do. After you make sure you have batteries in the house, you take a deep breath and get down to business. After all, replacing the batteries in some toys and games can bring a grown woman to her knees. After you searched high and low for the latch, button, or tab to open the battery compartment, none of the push, pull, slide actions seemed to work until finally . . . poof . . . you're in! You just hope you can remember what you did to close it back up again. But you're not out of the woods yet and you actually started to break out in a sweat as you stare at some battery that you swear you've never seen before. Off to the battery drawer; you hope you're not leading your child up to a big letdown. Searching and shuffling, you strike gold. You have one—just one—of these unique batteries. Quickly, you put it in and spend a few frustrating moments struggling to get the compartment closed again. Whew! Now you need a cocktail that will charge you up. Try The Fizzzbite martini that uses infused club soda for extra zing, kind of like getting a new battery installed.

 ## The Reward: *The Fizzzbite*

Makes 1 martini

> 1 ounces grappa
> Lemon-rosemary club soda, to fill
> Garnish: lemon wheel
> Garnish: rosemary sprig

Pour grappa in a shaker half filled with ice. Shake well and strain into a chilled martini glass. Fill with club soda, and garnish with lemon wheel and rosemary sprig.

The Dollhouse Martini

The Feat: *Helped Your Daughter Furnish Her Dollhouse*

Your daughter wanted to furnish her dollhouse. The only challenge was she had exquisite taste. When you looked at the big price for some of these mini tables, chairs, and desks, you almost passed out in the hobby shop aisle. Does anyone else realize that this furniture is for a dollhouse and not a real house? There had to be a different approach. You may not be Martha Stewart, but you're pretty good with a glue gun and a stapler. So you bought some scraps and end pieces of really nice fabric and worked with your daughter to re-cover some less expensive doll furniture. Not only did you save some money, but you got some quality time with your girl and taught her a lesson in value. When all was said and done, you and your girl had created a pretty swanky home setting for her little dolls. And, more importantly, she was happy. Now that she's busy playing, you need to reward yourself with a nice little cocktail that looks and tastes rich, but doesn't cost you an arm and a leg. Mix up the Bourbon Satin martini and sit back on some grown-up furniture to enjoy.

 The Reward: *Bourbon Satin*

Makes 1 martini

1½ ounces bourbon
1 ounce white crème de menthe
1 ounce light cream

Pour all ingredients into a shaker half filled with ice. Shake well and strain into a martini glass.

Refrigerator Art Martini

The Feat: *Made Macaroni Art*

What's more American than macaroni art? With all that white glue and curly noodles stuck to a paper plate or piece of construction paper, it just screams childhood arts and crafts project. You'd do almost anything for your little sweetheart, and when she asked you, "Pretty please, would you make a picture with her?" how could you say no? So glue, glitter, and some macaroni were spread out on the kitchen table, and you two got busy being creative. The fruits of your labor are now carefully drying and will end up in a spot of honor on the refrigerator door—where all things noteworthy live. The next time she wants you to participate in some kiddie arts and crafts project, you will absolutely pull out the paste and get to it. Speaking of American art and sweethearts, now is a great time to try the American Sweetheart martini. Kentucky bourbon and Southern Comfort combine with some vermouth and sweet-and-sour mix to create a lovely American original . . . just like your little girl. All you have to do is sip away while you deposit this day in your memory bank.

The Reward: *American Sweetheart*
Makes 1 martini

1 ounce bourbon
1 ounce Southern Comfort
Dash dry vermouth
Sweet-and-sour mix

Pour all ingredients into a shaker with ice. Shake well and strain into a chilled martini glass.

The Why Not Martini

The Feat: *Answered the Question "Why?" Umpteen Times in a Row*

You have to wonder if your kids keep asking, "Why?" because they really want to know or if they're just trying to push your buttons. Likely it's a bit of both, but today you just won both battles with your child. Yes, you actually lost count of how many times you heard the question, but you managed to stay cool and keep answering, time after time. Hopefully your kid actually gained some knowledge in this quirky question and answer game. But eventually, your tyke got tired of the back and forth and wandered off to play another game. All you know is now that it's over, you need a drink to clear your head. The Jamaican Me Crazy martini is perfect because, of course, that's what you really wanted to say to your child about halfway through the torrent of "whys"!

The Reward: *Jamaican Me Crazy*
Makes 1 martini

1 ounce light rum
1 ounce coconut rum
1 ounce banana liqueur
½ ounce cranberry juice
½ ounce pineapple juice
Garnish: 1 cherry

Pour all liquid ingredients into an ice-filled shaker. Shake and strain into a martini glass. Garnish with the cherry.

The Always Be Prepared Martini

The Feat: *Named Girl Scout Troop Leader*

It's time to brush up on your arts and crafts, because you were just named the new Girl Scout troop leader. Maybe you were asked before and declined, or this might be your first opportunity to support the scouts, but the timing seemed right. You thought about it and decided you were ready to step up to the plate and take on that multifaceted role. It's all about leading by example and walking the talk, right? Whether you were a Girl Scout yourself or not doesn't matter; you just need to do the best you can and look forward to all the fun you're going to have awarding those badges! From baking to fire building to civic responsibility and more, you get to be a part of helping young ladies—your own daughter included—discover their personal best. Oh, and did anyone mention the cookies? Now you get to order them, store them, sell them, distribute them, and, when no one is looking, eat them. Celebrate this delicious new responsibility with The Thin Mintini! Seriously, thin mints rule . . .

The Reward: *The Thin Mintini*

Makes 1 martini

1 ounce green crème de menthe
1 ounce Godiva Liqueur
1 ounce chocolate liqueur
1 ounce Irish cream liqueur
1 ounce cream

Pour all ingredients into an ice-filled shaker. Shake and strain into a chilled martini glass.

Tea for Two-tini

The Feat: *Attended Your Daughter's Tea Party*

An invitation was extended to you for an afternoon tea party, and it was a request you could not refuse. Your sweet little girl was hosting her first pretend tea party, and you wanted to be there to experience every moment. There was a list of chores as long as your arm that you had hoped to get done, but instead, you donned your best hat and gloves and joined your girl in her bedroom. Other guests included her favorite doll and stuffed toy, so you felt extremely privileged to be on the list. You enjoyed her air tea and invisible cookies with gusto while you chatted away with Mr. Bear and Dolly. All in all, it was not the worst conversation you had ever had. When tea time was over and your daughter moved on to reading a book, you slipped out to get going on your afternoon to-do list. But before you get too wrapped up in laundry and dusting, why not have some real tea? Sip an Electric Iced Teani while you reward yourself for spending the afternoon with your daughter.

The Reward: *Electric Iced Teani*

Makes 1 martini

½ **ounce vodka**	1 **ounce sour mix**
½ **ounce gin**	**Splash Sprite or 7 Up**
½ **ounce rum**	**Garnish: 1 maraschino cherry**
½ **ounce tequila**	**Garnish: orange wedge**
½ **ounce blue curaçao**	

Pour first 6 ingredients into a shaker half filled with ice. Shake well and strain into a chilled martini glass. Add splash of Sprite or 7 Up and garnish with cherry and orange wedge.

Electric Iced Teani

The Spa Day Martini

The Feat: *Let Your Daughter Do Your Hair and Makeup*

You're brave. You're daring. And you agreed to let your daughter do your hair and makeup. Seriously, it's not something every mom would say yes to, but you've always had an adventurous spirit. Besides, you made her promise there would be no scissors (or anything else that would permanently change your look) involved, so how bad could it really be? And maybe, just maybe, you'd like the results. So, your in-home beauty spa opened for business with you as the first customer. There was a flurry of activity with gels, mousses, sprays, powders, shadows, blush, and lipsticks flying about. Those giggles made you a tad nervous, but she wouldn't even let you have a peek until it was all complete. So you waited patiently, thumbing through some magazine. You chatted with her as she teased and combed and dabbed and daubed, realizing that this was one of those moments that you two would share forever. And when it was all done, it didn't matter if you looked like a queen or a tart; it was time with your girl that was the most beautiful thing . . . more priceless than jewels. So relish that moment with the Crown Jewel martini.

The Reward: *Crown Jewel*
Makes 1 martini

2½ ounces Malibu rum	Splash cranberry juice
2 ounces Crown Royal	Splash Sprite or 7 Up
Splash pineapple juice	Garnish: pineapple wedge

Pour first 4 ingredients into a shaker with ice. Shake and strain into a martini glass. Add a splash of Sprite or 7 Up and garnish with pineapple wedge.

Crown Jewel

Let's Pretend Martini

The Feat: *Played House with Your Daughter and Let Her Be the Mom*

Kids like to pretend, and the majority of their play is made up of pretending to be something they're not. Whether it's wanting to be cowboys, police, doctors, or vets, kids start out at a very young age pretending to be adults. Sometimes it sparks their passion for what they want to be when they grow up, but sometimes it's just a game. Today your little girl wanted to play house, but this time she wanted you to play with her while she was the mom. Having the tables turned on you can be interesting to say the least. You figured whatever mom she portrayed was probably a reflection of how she saw you. What if you didn't like it? What if you did? You agreed and spent some time being the child in your daughter's fantasy world. You were both proud and pleased with the kind, sweet mother your girl portrayed. That must have meant you were doing something right. Since her snack time was all pretend, why don't you fix yourself up with a real snack of the adult variety? Enjoy the Oatmeal Cookie martini that's a wonderful mix of coffee, crème, and cinnamon.

 The Reward: *Oatmeal Cookie*

Makes 1 martini

1½ **ounces Kahlúa**
1½ **ounces Baileys**
1½ **ounces Goldschläger**

Pour all ingredients into a shaker filled with ice. Shake and strain into a martini glass.

In-Home Movie Martini

The Feat: *Watched Your Kids' Favorite Movie with Them*

Your children absolutely love watching their favorite movie over and over again. and while you're so sick of watching that particular movie, you've decided you could handle watching the flick one more time if it meant that you'd get in some quality time with your kids. You even popped popcorn and had their favorite beverages to make it a real movie-going experience. You practiced your suspension of disbelief and tried to watch the movie through the eyes of your children. You were a bit surprised how much you enjoyed yourself, but that was in part because your kids were having such a great time. Admittedly, you found yourself longing for some real dialogue and a little less computer graphics. But as the saying goes, they don't make them like they used to. Maybe there would be a classic film on the movie channel you could watch after the kids went to bed. Meanwhile, you can ponder the future of the movie business while you taste a lovely little martini called The Hollywood. It has just three ingredients, much like a good film should have three acts. Shake, sip, and remember you're a star . . . a star of a mom!

The Reward: *The Hollywood*
Makes 1 martini

> **1 ounce vodka**
> **1 ounce raspberry liqueur**
> **Pineapple juice, to fill**
> **Garnish: pineapple chunks (optional)**

Pour the vodka and raspberry liqueur into a shaker half filled with ice. Shake and strain into a martini glass. Fill with pineapple juice. Garnish with pineapple chunk.

The Hollywood

Shop 'Til You Drop Martini

The Feat: *Went on a Mother-Daughter Shopping Spree and Stayed on Budget*

Admittedly you love shopping, and so does your girl. So a mother-daughter shopping spree seemed like a great bonding experience. The challenge, of course, was to stay on budget. Part of the fun of a shopping spree is acting like money doesn't matter and like you'd be going home to your Park Avenue penthouse. Therefore, too much worrying about what you were spending would take all the fun out of the day. But not enough attention to the sales slips would take the fun out of the rest of the month. So you struck a balance and took on the challenge of bargain hunting at the best stores. You and your child spent a bit more time window shopping and a lot more time looking at the closeout racks, but by the end of the day you both had a few great purchases and many more memories. Now that you're home soaking your tired, achy feet, you need to toast your economic brilliance and the end of another financially successful day as a mom. Why not live it up with a posh cocktail? The Park Avenue martini is a blend of gin, vermouth, and pineapple juice that lets you know you're living the sweet life.

The Reward: *Park Avenue*

Makes 1 martini

2 ounces gin
½ ounce dry vermouth
½ ounce sweet vermouth
½ ounce pineapple juice

Pour all ingredients into a shaker filled with ice. Shake and strain into a chilled martini glass.

That's My Toy Martini

The Feat: *Made It Out of the Store with the Year's Hot Brand-Name Toy*

You're finally back home after what felt an awful lot like going into battle. As you collapse on the sofa to survey your wounds (seriously that one spot where you got elbowed is probably going to bruise) you smile the smile of victory. You managed to brave the lines, endure the pushes and shoves, and purchase the brand-name toy of the season. This was your first winning toy-purchasing battle, and as you massage your aching feet, you're already imagining your kid's face when he unwraps this must-have item. Still, this venture is one you hope you don't have to repeat anytime soon. At least you won't lie awake at night worrying about what would happen if you didn't get one of these supplies-are-limited things. It was causing nightmares, but now it's all a dream come true for you and your child. As a part of your battle recovery, mix yourself up a Dream Martini and know you've fulfilled another wish. Go, Mom!

 The Reward: *Dream Martini*

Makes 1 martini

4 ounces brandy
1 ounce triple sec
½ ounce anisette

Pour ingredients into a shaker nearly filled with ice. Shake and strain into a martini glass.

Make It Yours Martini

The Feat: *Indulged Your Child's Wish for Their Bedroom Décor*

Maybe you're crazy, but it was just paint . . . for the most part. Letting your son pick out his room décor was actually a great way to let him express himself. And he promised to help with the transformation of his space. You knew the must-have colors and characters would only last for a while, and you would be stuck having to update, repaint, and redecorate down the road, but you also knew that the redo would make him happy and maybe, just maybe, encourage him to keep his room neater. So you took him to the home improvement store to pick paint and wallpaper. Armed with all the materials, including new bedding, the two of you went to work. Even though you ended up doing the bulk of it, you had some great quality time with your boy. As you stand back and admire the completed project, you really do hope this phase doesn't last too long. In recognition of your sanity (or the question of it), whip up an Asylum martini to sip. With this drink in your arsenal, you can survive any number of bedroom themes.

The Reward: *Asylum*

Makes 1 martini

> 2 ounces absinthe
> 2 ounces gin
> ½ ounce grenadine

Pour all ingredients into a shaker half filled with ice. Shake thoroughly and strain into a chilled martini glass.

Chapter 12

In the Great Outdoors Feats

These days getting kids to spend enough time outdoors can be a challenge. The great outdoors is competing with cable television, video games, computers, and all those bells, whistles, and flashing lights can be intoxicating. With all this going on, any day you can get your kids off the sofa and outside is a good day. And, Mom, you do a wonderful job of making those days happen just by taking your kids to the park or walking in the rain with them. And sometimes you can even get them outside to help with chores like raking leaves and cleaning out the car—and you even have a way of making those chore days super fun.

So thanks for rooting for your kids, taking the time to play in the park, and getting them to practice. But since you do so much for your kids, it's time to do something for you. This chapter includes some great martini recipes that you need to shake up and try. If the weather allows, why not take them outside and sip them on the back deck or patio?

The Feat: *Served as CEO of the Lemonade Stand*

Is there anything more exciting than watching your child dream about doing something new and exciting? That's especially true when your kid is planning her first venture into the world of business with the ever-popular lemonade stand. You were right there behind her as she made her signs and set up her table, helping just enough—but not too much. Your role was that of CEO, as you watched your fledgling entrepreneur take flight. Of course, she needed a loan from you to get things started and a little help actually making the lemonade was also in order. Still, once you fronted the money for the change box and helped carry out the product, like any good boss you faded into the background. You kept a watchful eye out, checked on the supply line as needed, and encouraged her throughout the day. When it was time to close shop for the night, you cheered her successes and downplayed any bumps along the way. That's good leadership—and good mothering. But you were left with lots of lemons and sugar. So what better way to get paid for all your hard work than with a citrusy sweet Lemon Drop martini? Good call.

The Reward: *Lemon Drop*

Makes 1 martini

> Sugar for rimming
> 1½ ounces citrus-flavored vodka
> ½ ounce triple sec or Cointreau
> 1 ounce lemon juice
> ½ ounce simple syrup
> Garnish: 1 sugar-coated lemon wedge

Rim a martini glass with sugar. Pour liquid ingredients into an ice-filled shaker. Shake and then strain into the glass. Garnish with a sugar-coated lemon wedge set on the rim.

Lemon Drop

Take It Outside Martini

The Feat: *Got the Kids to Play Outside*

Too much kid time? Too many days playing inside, rather than out? Relief is on the way. Finally, the sun is out and the temperature is warm enough to send kids into the yard. Now, how to get them there and away from the television or computer screen? Oh right, encourage them to get dirty (like they need any encouragement). Get out and make some mud pies, or sail paper boats in mud puddles, you suggest. Eventually, something you say works and they're off and running. Way to go! It feels like everyone's been cooped up for months, but maybe it's only been days. No matter, perception is reality and your reality is this . . . the kids are playing outside, and that means you are almost alone. Maybe you'll catch up on cleaning, watch your favorite movie, or just enjoy the quiet and take a nap. It's up to you, because you've already tackled your biggest hurdle . . . getting the children outside. But before you decide what to do, take a moment to toast yourself. In honor of the knowledge the kids will come back covered in mud, why not mix up a sweet, chocolate Mudslide Martini?

The Reward: *Mudslide Martini*
Makes 1 martini

Chocolate syrup
1 ounce vodka
1 ounce Irish cream liqueur
1 ounce coffee brandy
Garnish: whipped cream (optional)

Swirl chocolate syrup on the inside of a martini glass. Pour liquid ingredients into a shaker nearly filled with ice. Stir well and strain into the martini glass. Garnish with whipped cream if desired.

The Get 'er Done Martini

The Feat: *Survived a Jam-Packed Day of Soccer, Swimming, Etc.*

It was one of those days when you didn't stop moving all day. From the time you got the kids up in the morning to the time you tucked them back in bed at night, all you did was go, go, go! You started the day with the morning marathon of getting them out of bed, dressed, fed, and into the car for a day full of activities. Oh, and you remembered to check for everyone's gear, equipment, clothes, and shoes. Kids today are busier than ever, and the only person busier still is you . . . the mom who's getting them from point A to point B on time, every time (well almost every time—no one's perfect). Then when you finally got your children home, it was another meal, a check on homework, and back to bed with your hoping tomorrow would be a bit saner. Fully depleted from your day, you need to take in some nourishment. There's nothing wrong with having that nourishment—veggies and all—in a nice martini glass. So, get out the celery, shake up a Bloody Mary Martini and load up on vitamins.

The Reward: *Bloody Mary Martini*
Makes 1 martini

> **2 ounces vodka**
> **Bloody Mary mix, to fill**
> **Garnish: celery stalk**
> **Garnish: lime wedge**

Combine vodka and Bloody Mary mix in a shaker filled with ice. Shake and strain into a chilled martini glass. Garnish with a short stick of celery and lime wedge and anything else your heart desires.

Bloody Mary Martini

Anything You Can Do I Can Do Better-tini

The Feat: *Kept Up with Your Toddler on the Jungle Gym*

Park time with your toddler can be a blast, and watching him bravely go down the slide, climb through tunnels, and swing away surely makes you proud. You used to think watching was enough, but this time he wanted you to play with him. Not wanting to disappoint your acrobat, you stepped right up. You forgot how small they make monkey bars and jungle gyms, but what you really forgot was how exhausting all the playtime can be. Still, you hung in there, did your best, and managed to laugh it off when you got stuck on a slide built for tikes. After all, his giggles and smiles were enough to keep you going until it was finally time to head for home. He was ready for a nap and you were ready for a hot bath and a great cocktail! Sounds like good medicine for some well-earned relaxation! Even if you don't have time for the bath, you can still sip the perfect cocktail for your day on the monkey bars: the Monkey Gland martini.

The Reward: *Monkey Gland*
Makes 1 martini

2 ounces gin
1 ounce orange juice
1 dash Pernod
¼ ounce grenadine
Garnish: 1 orange twist

Pour all liquid ingredients into a strainer half filled with ice. Shake and strain into a martini glass. Garnish with an orange twist.

Magic Moments Martini

The Feat: *Planted an Herb Garden with Your Kid*

Spending the afternoon digging in the dirt and planting seeds can be very rewarding and it's even better when you get to do it with your child, like you did today when you planted some herbs for your window box. You decided it was also a great opportunity to teach your kid a bit about where your food comes from and how important it is to take care of the earth. Growing something together will give you time to bond for weeks and months as you tend your mini-crop together. If all goes well, you'll soon have some parsley and sage to use in your cooking, which will provide even more opportunities to teach your kid some lessons and skills to use later in life. And an afternoon well spent deserves a happy hour well served. In honor of your time spent in the garden, mix up this tequila-based Jumping Beans martini. Maybe later you'll tell your child the story of Jack and the Beanstalk and talk about the lessons learned in that tale, but for now, enjoy this fun martini.

 The Reward: *Jumping Beans*
Makes 1 martini

3 ounces aged tequila
1 ounce sambuca
3 coffee beans

Pour the tequila and sambuca into a martini glass and drop in the coffee beans.

The Giddy Up Martini

The Feat: *Ponied Up for Horseback Riding Lessons*

Your daughter is obsessed with horses—just like you were at the same age. Now you have something else in common with your growing girl and a great way to relate to her. However, the challenge was getting her riding lessons. After all, nothing is cheap these days and horseback riding lessons can be on the pricey side. You studied your budget, looked at expenses, and through some mom-style creativity, you figured out a way to make your child's dreams come true. Ever since you told her the good news, she's been bouncing off the walls. It's a happy night in the house, and soon conversations will lead to all things horses. Enjoy this time and celebrate a win in the mom column. Now it's time for you to do a little something for yourself. Fancy it up with a little brandy and Benedictine and you've got the horse-themed martini called The Preakness. All you have to do now is curl up on the sofa with this horsey cocktail and watch *Black Beauty*.

 ## The Reward: *The Preakness*
Makes 1 martini

> 3 ounces blended whiskey
> 1 ounce Benedictine
> ½ ounce brandy
> 2 dashes bitters
> Garnish: lemon twist

Pour all ingredients, except garnish, into a shaker half filled with ice. Shake well and strain into a martini glass. Garnish with a lemon twist.

Where In the World Is . . . My Martini

The Feat: *Played Hide-and-Seek*

You had a long list of chores to do, but your kid was playing solo that day and soon got bored. That's how you got roped into playing hide-and-seek when you didn't really have the extra time. Instead of worrying about all those undone projects, you decided to just stop and be in the moment. You could play hide-and-seek with the best of them, so you opted to brush up on your skills and get to hiding, or seeking, depending on who was doing what. The fun thing for you was to pretend you couldn't find your child, even long after you knew exactly the chosen hiding spot. Once again, Mom, you put your child first and made some great memories along the way. Much like hide-and-seek, sometimes great moments are hidden away in ordinary days. To celebrate these great moments, sit down with a Velvet Hammer martini. The crisp vodka is hidden by the sweet crème de cacao and smooth cream. So when you taste this one, remember what's hiding in that creamy goodness.

The Reward: *Velvet Hammer*
Makes 1 martini

> 1½ ounces vodka
> 1 tablespoon crème de cacao
> 1 tablespoon cream

Pour all ingredients into a shaker with ice. Shake and strain into a martini glass.

The Fall Has Fell Martini

The Feat: *Raked the Yard with Your Kids*

Autumn is a wonderful time of year with the crisp air and beautiful fall foliage everywhere. The problem with those gorgeous leaves of red, yellow, and gold is that eventually they fall into your yard. But even raking leaves can be fun! You gathered up your young ones, lightly bundled them up against the breeze, and put a rake in each of their hands. If everyone worked together it would take so much less time, and you promised them a fun surprise later. Sure enough, you and your kids soon had the yard whipped into shape with a large pile of leaves ready to go. Then came the surprise . . . you got a running start and jumped right into the middle of the pile. It took little to no encouragement for your kids to try it with you. Soon you were all laughing and rolling around in the brightly colored heap of fall fun, which you had raked back up in no time flat! At day's end you can check that to-do off your list and relax with the aptly named Autumn in New York martini.

 ## The Reward: *Autumn in New York*
Makes 1 martini

> **1 ounce applejack brandy**
> **½ ounce Tuaca**
> **Hot apple cider, to fill**
> **Garnish: whipped cream**

Pour the applejack brandy and Tuaca in a room-temperature, or warmed, martini glass and carefully fill with hot apple cider. Garnish with whipped cream.

Raindrops Keep Falling on My . . . Martini

The Feat: *Played in the Rain Without an Umbrella*

Being spontaneous can sometimes create the best memories. That's what happened when you decided to go for a walk with your kid. You were halfway through your stroll when the rain started. You'd meant to grab the umbrellas, but that didn't happen. So did you rush home and get out of the rain or did you relax and have fun? Option number two, please! You and your child decided to splash in puddles and just play in the rain all the way home. Who cares if you got soaked to the bone! A warm shower and a blanket on the sofa will fix that up in no time at all. Besides, when is the last time you got to just enjoy being with your kid—or acted like a kid for that matter? After some good playtime, the two of you stumble and squish into the house, laughing the entire time. Congratulations, Mom, on making the most of the moment. Now, how about a rain-themed martini? Tropical Rainstorm comes with cherry brandy and that'll warm you straight to your bones.

The Reward: *Tropical Rainstorm*
Makes 1 martini

1½ ounces dark rum
1 teaspoon triple sec
½ ounce cherry brandy
½ ounce lemon juice

Pour all ingredients into a shaker half filled with ice. Shake well and strain into a martini glass.

The Tiny Bubbles Martini

The Feat: *Blew Bubbles for Thirty Minutes Straight*

Making kids laugh and smile is addictive. Do it once and you'll try and try again to make them do it again, which often means repeating an activity over and over (and over) again. This time it was blowing bubbles. All in all not the worst activity to put on the repeat cycle, but today you blew bubbles for thirty minutes straight. You did your best to continue to look interested and, of course, seeing that smile and hearing that giggle kept you going. Finally something else got the focus and you were able to stop. Good thing too, because you were almost out of bubble juice. Speaking of bubble juice, your efforts deserve a little themed reward. And you probably need to replenish energy as well. Here's just the thing to do both. Get out the bottle of champagne hidden in the back of the fridge, add a little tangerine vodka and tangerine juice (that's the energy), and take a sip. The aptly named Tangerine Bubbles martini might even make *you* giggle a bit.

The Reward: *Tangerine Bubbles*
Makes 1 martini

> 2 ounces tangerine vodka
> 2 ounces fresh tangerine juice
> Dry champagne, to fill

Pour the vodka and juice into a martini glass, and then fill with the dry champagne. Stir slightly.

Tangerine Bubbles

The Feat: *Reminded Yourself That Your Son Is Probably Not the Next Olympic Swimming Sensation*

You hated to think it, and there's no way you were ready to say it out loud, but at the end of another swim meet the reality was there. Your son, as much as he loved swimming, was probably not the next Michael Phelps, Olympic wonder, swimmer extraordinaire. Yes, your son was pretty good and had managed to win a few races, but you knew it was wise to keep your hopes and expectations in check. You let go of that dream of having his gold medal framed and hanging on the mantel and just focused on supporting him. The cool thing is that while that reality was there, you never let it dampen your encouragement. With all expectations out of the way, you were free to cheer for your boy, even scream at the top of your lungs once in a while. And who needs prime seats at the Olympics in ten years when you can enjoy a great Olympic Martini right now. A little brandy, triple sec, and OJ make the cocktail of champions!

The Reward: *Olympic Martini*

Makes 1 martini

1½ **ounces brandy**
1½ **ounces triple sec**
1½ **ounces orange juice**

Pour all ingredients into a shaker with ice. Shake and strain into a martini glass.

Fake It 'Til You Make It Martini

The Feat: *Filled In as Coach on the T-Ball Team*

You're not really sure how it happened, but somehow you were elected/named/volunteered-to-fill-in-as coach of the T-ball team. Whether you played T-ball as a kid, or softball or baseball later on didn't seem to factor into the process. So you put on your game face and got to work. Luckily, you remembered that it was just T-ball and realized that just getting these little tykes to pay attention through an entire game was considered a success. It was all about having fun and learning about good sportsmanship, not about winning the game. Yes, you may have had a rough start, but you hung in there. You worked with those wee ones and did the best you could. In the end, it seemed like a good time was had by all. So hang up your cleats, hit the showers, and then sit down and taste the goodness that is The Rough Start martini. It's a yummy blend of apples and bourbon that's sure to warm you up and keep you in the game.

 ## The Reward: *The Rough Start*

Makes 2 martinis

Juice of ½ lemon
4 ounces apple cider
2 ounces bourbon
1 ounce apple brandy

Pour all ingredients into a shaker filled with ice. Shake well and strain into chilled martini glasses.

Out on a Limb Martini

The Feat: *Helped Your Kids Build a Tree House*

Your kids thought you were Supermom, and you know that you can do anything—almost. You had never built a tree house before, but why should that stop you from trying? So, with some online research, a trip to the home improvement store, and a few helpful hints from someone there, you headed home to help your kids build a tree house. It may have taken a bit longer than you had hoped, but you wanted to be sure it was done right. If your kids were going to be up in this thing, you were going to be sure it was sturdy. With only a few minor mishaps, the tree house was done. The kids were up in it and playing and you were safely back on the ground in a lounge chair. Maybe you aren't Supermom, but you aren't afraid to try new things. And, that's a value you want to be sure your kids learn well. So take your bandaged fingers (there were some minor mishaps) and get inside to mix yourself up a Chick's Fix martini. After all, you've earned it!

 ## The Reward: *Chick's Fix*
Makes 1 martini

Juice from ½ lemon or lime
1 teaspoon powdered sugar
1 teaspoon water
1½ ounces coconut rum
1 ounce pineapple vodka
Garnish: lemon slice

Pour all ingredients, except garnish, into a shaker half filled with ice. Shake well and strain into a chilled martini glass. Garnish with a lemon slice.

Cruising for a Martini

The Feat: *Talked Your Kids Into Helping You Clean Out the Car*

A car can only take so much before it just has to be cleaned out. And since the kids are responsible for at least fifty percent of the mess (okay maybe more), it only makes sense that they help clean it out, however unwilling they may be. Because you're brilliant, you've found ways to motivate them to help. Maybe it was the guarantee they could keep all the loose change they found, or maybe it was the promise of their favorite fast-food treat, or a prize for the one who found the missing math book, but you found their secret inspiration and it worked. In no time at all, every stray pencil, notebook, coat, shoe, and toy was out of the car. You could actually see the floorboards again, which made vacuuming so much easier. Score another one for you in getting the kids to help with yet another chore. In honor of your victory—and in honor of a clean car—shake up a nice clean, crisp Gin Gimlet Martini!

 The Reward: *Gin Gimlet Martini*

Makes 1 martini

> **4 ounces gin**
> **1½ ounces sweetened lime juice (or fresh lime juice and simple syrup)**
> **Garnish: lime wedge**

Pour the gin and lime juice in a shaker filled with ice. Shake and strain into a martini glass. Garnish with lime wedge.

I'm a Rock Star-tini

The Feat: *Chaperoned Daughter and Friends at Boy Band Concert*

Ever since Elvis, girls have been screaming and swooning over young, cute music men (boys). It's a part of growing up and darn near a rite of passage. You went through it, and now your daughter is doing the same. But another rite of passage belongs to parents, those who get the special duty of chaperoning a gaggle of giggling girls to a concert for their favorite boy band. This time it was your turn! You promised not to embarrass your daughter, so you were sneaky about the earplugs and tried not to let them see you smirk or roll your eyes. Hey, you even splurged and bought a few overpriced posters and T-shirts to help them to remember the big night. Now that you're home and your ears have almost stopped ringing, congratulate yourself for making it through the mania. Remember who your biggest musical crush was on and reminisce a little. While you're at it, enjoy the Pop Star martini. This slightly retro cocktail is light and sweet, like most pop music, with a dash of candy to make it fizzle and zap.

 The Reward: *Pop Star*

Makes 1 martini

1 packet of strawberry Pop Rocks
2 ounces strawberry vodka
1 ounce fresh lemon juice
1 ounce simple syrup
Garnish: 1 star fruit slice

Rim a martini glass with Pop Rocks. Pour all liquid ingredients into a shaker with ice. Shake and strain into the Pop Rock–rimmed martini glass. Garnish with the star fruit slice.

About the Authors

Rose Maura Lorre blogtends FiveOClockCocktails.com and is the food critic for *St. Louis Magazine*. She has tended bar at the Royale Food & Spirits in St. Louis and is a graduate of the Columbia University School of Mixology. Rose has celebrated bylines in the *New York Times*, *Entertainment Weekly*, *Time Out New York*, *Glamour*, *Men's Health*, *Marie Claire*, *Cosmopolitan*, *Maxim*, the *New York Post*, *New York Daily News*, Salon.com, and *Seattle Weekly*. In 2005, the Association of Food Journalists awarded her First Place for Best Restaurant Criticism. Her blog was a finalist for the Saveur 2012 Best Food Blog Awards. She and her husband, Sean, just welcomed their first child. They live in Montreal, Quebec.

Mavis Lamb began her career in Los Angeles as a film production coordinator during the 1980s heyday of music videos. She later moved on to Nashville to produce music videos for several country artist greats before settling in Seattle as a script writer and PR chick. These days she coaches people on blogging for business, speaks on networking and word-of-mouth marketing, and writes books and plays. As director of Seattle Playwrights Studio, her latest play *Serendipity by Design* was inspired by a conversation with her boyfriend, Dave, a martini bar owner.